AF251235

IF THE BIBLE IS REALLY TRUE…
You Could Be In Big Trouble!

By

Ralph Filicchia

Scripture taken from the New King James Version. Copyright 1982 by Thomas Nelson, Inc. Used by permission. All rights reserved.

ISBN 0-7414-1332-9

Published by:

INFINITY
PUBLISHING.COM

519 West Lancaster Avenue
Haverford, PA 19041-1413
Info@buybooksontheweb.com
www.buybooksontheweb.com
Toll-free (877) BUY BOOK
Local Phone (610) 520-2500
Fax (610) 519-0261

Printed in the United States of America

Printed on Recycled Paper

Published March, 2004

Contents

PREFACE

Religion can be boring, fascinating, tiresome, a drag, stimulating, murderous, a necessary bother, satisfying, comforting, divisive, a cause of war, an instrument of healing, something that can lead you to Heaven when you die, or to Hell where you will suffer forever.

"Whoa, just a minute here. Religion can lead you to Hell? What are you talking about? Religion is good. God is all in favor of religion. There's no such thing as bad religion."

Sorry, pal, but religion can lead you to Hell. All you have to do is get involved with the wrong one. If there is only one true God, then there can only be one true religion. False religion does no one any good.

Mother Teresa was once asked, "Do you try to convert to Catholicism those in other religions when you minister to them?"

She answered, "No, we feel it is better to leave them in the religion in which they feel comfortable."

If the Bible is really true as written—doing this could be deadly!

Does this sound un-American? Does it seem somewhat discriminatory or offensive? Don't worry about it. You are not about to read a politically--or religiously--correct book. You are not about to read a book that has been Americanized. You are not about to read a book whose aim is to inspire the reader, or make his life more meaningful, or solve his problems, or teach him the biblical way of losing weight, etc. We have already been flooded with enough of this stuff.

The purpose of this book is to lay certain truths on the line as they have already been revealed, and to demolish some misconceptions that have done untold damage to millions.

Some of these truths may not be popular, many will not be believed, and some might be fanatically opposed.

But if they are true according to the Bible, well....

INTRODUCTION

Have you ever had someone say to you, "All your religious ideas are based on blind faith?"

I have, and I must admit that at one time the accusation bothered me. Was I blindly following that which I could not prove? I could not with a pencil and paper prove the existence of God; I could not prove to a skeptic's satisfaction that there was once a man named Cain who killed his brother Abel; I could not prove that Moses once parted the Red Sea; and I could not prove that Jesus at one time fed five thousand people with a few fish and a few loaves of bread.

I was accepting all this on blind faith…or was I?

I began to analyze my position, and the more I thought about it the more I realized I was selling myself short.

The Christian faith is not based on blind faith—it is based on historical fact! It's history. The human race has done a fairly commendable job of recording its past, and the biblical writers have also done a very good job from their perspective.

Archaeology continues to support much of the Old Testament record at an increasing rate, and the prophecies of Christ in the New Testament concerning end times are being foreshadowed in the headlines of our daily newspapers.

I began to see that there was nothing "blind" about any of this. Certain things happened at a certain time in history and were recorded. What Moses, Jeremiah, and Jesus said and did was written down.

In the same sense, what Alexander the Great, Julius Caesar, Marco Polo, Christopher Columbus, and Benjamin Franklin said and did was also written down.

Is there any difference?

Not really. It's all recorded history. If we believe what someone wrote about Marco Polo, then why shouldn't we believe what someone wrote about Jesus Christ? If we believe that Alexander the Great conquered Persia and marched all the way to India, why shouldn't we believe that Moses led Israel out of Egypt and into the promised land?

Is there really any difference?

Well…there is one difference. In the biblical record we are acknowledging the existence of God. But some people find His existence disconcerting. They don't want to bother with God, and the best way to rid themselves of Him is to deny the authenticity of the record in which He is personified. If that record is not true, then He is not true, and of course those who believe in untrue records are guilty of blindly following that which has no basis in fact. If you persist in this then you are being guided by blind faith.

But I refuse to be pushed around in this manner by those whose thinking is weak and inconsistent. If I were to ask, "How do you know that in 44 B.C. Julius Caesar took control of Rome and proclaimed himself Dictator For Life?" the answer would be "It's in the history books."

Let's suppose I then ask, "Well who wrote the history book in which this is recorded?" To this question I can assure you there would be a long, if not never-ending silence. Rarely does anyone know the author of history books he read in school.

If this is not an example of blind faith, then I don't know what is. This person is guilty of taking something at face value without investigating the source of his information. Since no one ever questioned this before, then why should he?

Yet when I claim that Jesus Christ rose from the dead— a fact that had hundreds of eyewitnesses and that was recorded by a number of men—I am told that what I believe is being taken on blind faith.

But what is blind about believing a recorded historical fact? If I cannot believe that, then what right do you have believing that Ferdinand Magellan sailed from Seville, Spain, around the tip of South America to the Pacific Ocean? What right do you have in believing that Joan of Arc was burned at the stake?

In fact, to be blunt, you have no right to seriously believe anything that happened in the past. If historical fact does not exist for me, then why should it for you?

Believing that God spoke in times past to the fathers by the prophets, and in these last days has spoken to us by His son (Heb. 1:1), has more legitimacy than believing that man evolved from something floating in a prehistoric puddle all the way up to an ape and then to a man. There was no eyewitness to this happening. No one recorded it. There is no real proof of any kind that it ever happened.

Yet millions of people believe it. That, my friend, is blind faith!

But there is recorded history that God spoke to the Old Testament prophets, and there is recorded history that tells us Jesus claimed to speak with the authority of His heavenly Father. That is historical fact!

The Bible is, among other things, a very reliable history book. To doubt the events it records is not a very intelligent move. The book has too much going for it.

Blind faith should be reserved for those who haven't the faintest idea of why they hold to particular beliefs apart from the excuse that everyone else always believed them and it seemed the popular and intellectually safe thing to do.

However, people do not become Christians because it is an intellectually safe thing to do, or because everyone else is doing it. They become Christians because their hearts and minds were challenged by facts that could be dealt with no other way. This is not the result of "blindly" following anything.

It is the non-believer who is the practitioner of blind faith. He buys into opinions and philosophies with little regard for their source, and will tenaciously adhere to that which cannot be proved, historically or otherwise.

The truth of the Bible can be seen in the lives of those who have accepted and live by its precepts and doctrines. Those who are unaware of this, and who live by some other unproved or nonfactual belief, are the ones who live by blind faith.

THE BIBLE

If The Bible Is Really True…is a question of utmost importance. If it is not completely true, if it is just a nice religious book filled with some good advice that one can take or leave, then nothing that follows is of any real importance. It's just another religious book of which the world has many. If you find something in it that you feel is inspiring or helpful, that's good. If you don't, then don't worry about it.

But, if the Bible is true…then you, your family, and possibly most of your friends, could right now be in very serious trouble.

But before we go any further it will be necessary to define and explain the character of the Bible itself. Exactly what is it?

First of all, the Bible is not a book that was written (as most books are) from beginning to end by one person over a period of time.

No, the Bible is a collection of books and letters that were written over a period of roughly 1600 years by 40+ writers. These writers came from a variety of backgrounds. Some were kings, others shepherds; some were prophets, others were uneducated fishermen; at least one was a physician, and still others were tax collectors, scholars, priests, etc.

The Bible contains two volumes, the Old Testament and the New Testament. The Old Testament, stretching from

Genesis to the book of Malachi, is made up of 39 books and constitutes the first and larger section of the Bible.

The New Testament, beginning with Matthew and ending with Revelation, is composed of 27 books and letters and makes up the second and smaller section of the Bible. (In the complete King James Version of the Bible there are 791,328 words.)

Yet with all this variety of time, geography, and authorship, there remains the strong evidence of one author, as there is continuity of thought, harmony of purpose, perfection of detail, and lack of doctrinal contradiction.

In this one volume called the Bible we have (1) The law of Moses, (2) The history of Israel, (3) The Psalms of David, (4) The writings of the prophets, (5) The gospel of Jesus Christ, (6) The theology of the Apostle Paul, (7) And the Revelation of the end times written by John. All these sections together are in perfect harmony and accord.

Which of course then leads one to conclude, as do many of the biblical authors, that the Bible is not just the words of many different men, but is over and above that—also the very Word of God. Men were moved (inspired) to write so man would have a written guide for life in this world and a guidebook that can lead him to Heaven when he dies. "All Scripture is given by inspiration of God…" (2 Tim. 3:16), "…holy men of God spoke as they were moved by the Holy Spirit" (2 Pet. 1:21b).

The Old Testament is composed of three major divisions: the Law, the Psalms, and the Prophets. The first five books of Moses, Genesis-Exodus-Leviticus-Numbers and Deuteronomy are called The Law. The Psalms were composed mostly by David, and the Prophets cover the last seventeen books of the Old Testament, from the majesty of Isaiah to the small book of Malachi.

Plus there are historical books, the very unique book of Job, and others that stand by themselves. A number of times Jesus loosely referred to the whole Old Testament as "the Law and the Prophets" (Matt. 5:17-7:12).

Almost all of this material deals with the nation of Israel. Abraham was called by God (Gen. 12:1-3) and from Abraham came the Jewish nation. Abraham is the most pivotal individual in the Old Testament, and his life and faith carry all the way into Christian theology. "And if you are Christ's, then you are Abraham's seed, and heirs according to the promise" (Gal. 3:29).

When it comes to Christian theology Abraham is the man to watch in the Old Testament. Not Moses, not David, not Joshua, not Solomon—but Abraham! New Testament writers teach that if the believer relates to Jesus Christ the same way Abraham related to God in the Old Testament, he is on the right track. All other tracks lead to disaster (cf. Rom. 4 and Gal. 3,4).

"Wait a minute! What do you mean, all other tracks lead to disaster?"

They do. Do you know of some other biblical plan by which sinners can find a right relationship with God?

"Well…no, I'm no Bible expert."

Then stay with me and try to learn something.

The New Testament's main divisions are the Four Gospels: Matthew, Mark, Luke and John; the historical book of Acts; and the epistles and letters of the Apostle Paul and others.

The Gospels proclaim Christ. They record His words, His miracles, His teachings. They give vivid accounts of both His birth and His death. And they are historically accurate.

But it is the epistles that fully explain what the gospels dutifully proclaim. Especially the epistles of the Apostle Paul and most notably his epistle to the Romans—in which lies the very heart of Christian theology. In this epistle the sinful heart of man is described, analyzed, positioned for damnation, then miraculously saved through the intervention of Christ. Assuming, of course, that the individual sinner takes intelligent advantage of the plan of salvation the Apostle Paul presents.

If the Apostle Paul knows exactly what he's talking about (and the importance of this "if" will run throughout this book), then what he has written becomes the most important literature ever penned by any man.

Some literature inspires for a time, other literature informs, some entertains; some written words cause wars, other written words end them. But how many have ever written words whose impact will determine for millions whether or not they will spend eternity in Heaven, in the joy and presence of God, or suffer the anguish of the damned in Hell, the outer darkness, where there will be "weeping and gnashing of teeth" (Matt. 25:30) forever!

This literature (the Bible) is evidently the most meaningful literature ever written. Its value is beyond comprehension.

Of course, *if* it is not true, you would be foolish to worry about anything we have just discussed.

But if it is true, or the possibility exists, as far as you know, that it *might* be true....

Well...maybe you should settle back and start paying close attention.

THE GOD OF THE BIBLE

The Bible's main character is God. He is its overpowering presence from beginning to end. The Bible begins with "In the beginning God…" (Gen. 1:1) and ends with the declaration by Jesus Christ, the Son of God, "Surely I am coming quickly" (Rev. 22:20).

But just who is God?

Stop and think for a moment. God. A being who created everything we know and see. A conscious entity who claims to have always existed, and who loves with great love the crown jewel of His creation, man.

It actually strains the imagination to consider someone like this. How does He exist and where did He come from? If He really loves people and is so concerned about them then why doesn't he show Himself more openly?

And why does He allow so much misery in this world?

"Yeah, good question. Where was God when the World Trade Center was attacked on 9-11? Everybody's asking that question, but I don't hear anyone answering it."

All right, I'll give you the answer. He was right there beside you and I watching the whole spectacle, except that He probably didn't need TV to see what was going on. And the next question is…?

"Well then how come He didn't do anything to stop it?"

That's just the question I was expecting, and that's why the first question is never answered, because no one wants to tackle the second one. Many evangelical preachers, and especially liberal preachers, dance around this with a lot of philosophical mumbo-jumbo and seminary-speak that leaves you with more questions than you had before you went to hear them. So permit me to straighten you out:

The question is, "Why didn't God do anything to stop it?" and the answer is, "God did not stop it for the same reason He did not stop your Uncle Joe from dying of cancer, or the little girl two blocks down the street from getting run over by a bulldozer, or the earthquake in East Overshoe from killing 3000 people, or the flood in Southeast Asia from drowning 4000 people, or the bus accident from killing three families on their way to a church picnic, etc.

What I am saying is, this isn't Paradise, so don't expect the rules of Paradise to be in effect here. This is the world, and in this world there is a ruler, and his name is Satan. Didn't Jesus refer to Satan by this title in John 14:30 and 16:11? And doesn't it say in 1 John 5:19 that "the whole world lies under the sway (influence) of the wicked one? And didn't Satan himself say in Luke 4:6 that the authority and glory of this world's kingdoms had been delivered to him?

Simply put, the Devil has a lot to say about what goes on down here, and he influences much of what happens.

"Well what about these Christians who are always running around saying that God is in control?"

They are only partially right. Remember old Job in the Old Testament? He got hammered left and right. His kids were killed, his livestock was destroyed, and the poor guy ended up sitting in the dirt covered with painful boils.

Where was God? He was right there, just like He was on 9-11. He allows Satan, to an extent, to run wild, because, as we have just mentioned—this sinful world is his kingdom! And in his kingdom he goes about like a roaring lion seeking whom he may devour (cf. 1 Pet. 5:8)

So watch out, and learn how to live defensively!

But getting back to the God of the Bible, how do we know that He isn't just an invention of religious people who need some kind of crutch to lean on when the going gets tough?

Just who is God?

For many people God is the equivalent of X the unknown. He is some distant power in the sky vaguely associated with churches. He is something good like the American flag, Thanksgiving, and loving your neighbor. He is that which people associate with waving fields of grain, the One who gives rain to the crops, and who smiles on little kids as they play and experience the wonders and sights of life all around them, bugs, birds and airplanes.

And most comforting of all (they think), He is a wonderful person who forgives all our little misdeeds because, after all, no one is perfect. They acknowledge this God by attending church on Sundays, and by public statements at noteworthy events. God is to be believed in, trusted, and leaned upon in times of great crisis, because if we could not believe, trust, and lean on Him at times like that…who else is there?

They teach their children to behave properly because that is what God expects of them, and besides, they don't want their children ending up in jail, or worse. When someone dies they attend the funeral and listen respectfully as a clergyman sees the departed off into the next life. By their presence and solemn agreement with what is being said they acknowledge the existence of God.

To them God is the friend of the good guy, of the wonderful woman, of the heck of a nice kid. These people will eventually meet their God and find their eternal rest. And why shouldn't they? Aren't most people basically good?

If someone in their family comes down with a killer disease, or gets racked up in an accident and is rushed to the hospital, they are quick to pray to this God. When family members are uptight about another member of the family dying God becomes an item of general discussion.

"If God wants to take him then there's not much we can do," is a comment we often hear. Or, "If it's God's will…."

The idea of God has always been a comfort to those in collective sorrow. He is the last refuge and the final arbiter of life and death. In these times it is good that He exists. This is what God is all about; this is His time on the center stage of our lives.

But when times are good God reverts back to being that distant power in the sky, equivalent to the flag we see so often it becomes a bore to acknowledge. God is up there and doesn't bother us as long as we are not like Joe Stalin, Hitler, Muslim terrorists, or thieving dentists and mad serial killers. As long as we pay our bills and treat one another decently there is no real need to become more involved with Him.

There are some, fortunately or unfortunately (depending upon how you look at it), who do become more involved. We consider them, for the most part, to be a pain in the neck, bothersome, and even dangerous. There is nothing worse (as we are constantly reminded) than a religious fanatic. They are always quoting the Bible or talking about their church, always bothering people about their religion. We really don't understand why they are like that, because we all worship the same God anyway, don't we?

But do we?

Or better yet, is the God we have been talking about the same God who has revealed himself in the Bible? Isn't it only right that we should examine this God in light of what the Bible teaches, since, after all, this is the only place where He is directly quoted and where He speaks about himself?

All right, let's hear what the God of the Bible has to say about himself.

Immediately we run into trouble. The average person does not enjoy listening to Bible quotes. Bible quotes are synonymous with leather-lunged, street-corner preachers who want to make sure the heathen in India can hear their every word from thousands of miles away. Bible quotes are also the tools of those noisy aggravating people who want to "shove their religion down everyone else's throat."

So for the moment we will not quote the Bible. But we can safely say that, no matter what Bible translation you use (even some of the worthless modern ones), God does say in the Bible that (1) all men (and women) are sinners, (2) He judges sin, and (3) that He will send unrepentant (unsaved) sinners to Hell.

If the Bible does not say this then it does not say anything!

There is no possible way that the honest reader can avoid these three simple facts. To gloss over them with a false emphasis on God's love is nothing more than theological sabotage. God does send people to Hell. "And anyone not found written in the Book of Life was cast into the lake of fire" (Rev. 20:15).

But now we run into more trouble. Suddenly we are no longer talking about the good God who listens to our sobbing about the latest death in the family, hurricane disaster, or plane crash, and who then kindly steps out of the picture after we're through with Him…or who just shows up for funerals because that's His job.

No, we are now moving a bit beyond that to a God who is beginning to lean a bit heavy on us, and most people don't go for that.

"Well what's His complaint? Who's He mad at?"

Well, it seems He might be mad at us.

"Yeah, but wait a minute. I've always heard that God is a God of love. How about that, huh?"

All right, God is a God of love. In fact the Bible even says that God is love. But when discussing God we have to balance Him the way the Bible balances Him. In other words, you can't take one thing the Bible says about God and ignore other things. According to the Bible, God is a God of love, mercy, truth, justice, vengeance, wrath, and holiness. Plus, He is even a jealous God who does not put up with competition. Now how do you like that?

So to take just one attribute of God and ignore the rest will give us a distorted view of just who God is.

But this is something many people purposely avoid. It is obviously more comfortable to pick the attributes of God that we like and ignore the ones that make us uncomfortable. In this way it is easier to control God, to make Him more utilitarian, and at the same time maintain our independence—which in essence actually displaces Him.

In this sense, then, God is no longer God. He is instead a figment of our imagination, a useful by-product of our natural religious drives. He comes on the scene when we call, and then leaves when we are through with Him. He is a wonderful convenience.

But when we examine the total picture, as illustrated in the Bible, we do not find this God. Instead we come back to the God who has a complaint with us. The God who makes us uncomfortable. The God who won't be used or pushed around. The God who makes us wary of religion...the God who cramps our style.

Like it or not, the God of the Bible is not so much interested in our social problems (the homeless, AIDS, pollution, the environment, the cost of medicine, violence in the movies and on TV, etc.) as much as He is in individual morality, basic right and wrong, truth and error, and Right religion versus Wrong religion.

Most people are not too concerned with those last two listings. Right and Wrong religion depends upon how one looks at it, and truth and error are elastic terms. Nothing, they say, is really that cut and dried.

But the God of the Bible doesn't see it that way. He is for the most part an absolutist who has a tendency to see things in black and white. If He says something is wrong, then it's wrong, and that's it! There is no discussion, and you can forget about what the latest polls and studies have shown.

God will (mercifully) bend if you bend first, but His principles never change. His standards of right and wrong seem to remain constant and stay that way regardless of the latest trends.

There are some misguided Christians who teach that God is so perfect He never changes His mind. But that is not true. God is perfect, but the Bible is filled with instances where He changed His mind because He was asked to. The most notable example is found in 2 Kings 20:1-6 when God told Hezekiah he was going to die, and then because of Hezekiah's prayer and tears God changed His mind and told him he would be healed and live another fifteen years.

What then do we do with this God? We have three choices: We can deny His existence; we can refashion Him according to our likes and desires; or we can take Him as is and very seriously.

If we deny His existence we stand a good chance of ending up in an eternally disastrous situation called Hell. (The empty arguments of those who say a God of love would never send anyone to Hell have to be discarded if we are to take the Bible with any degree of significance.)

If we fashion Him according to our desires we are still denying Him, which will of course bring the same results.

If we take Him seriously we are faced with at least one obligation, and here we must break our rule and quote a Bible verse. The writer in Ecc. 12:13 says, "The conclusion, when all has been heard, is, Fear God and keep His commandments."

That seems simple enough…and also safe when we consider the alternative.

But when we look around our world we don't find many people doing this. The world seems to be a madhouse with wars and murders and terrorism and grand theft, etc., everywhere we turn. The Bible states: "Truly the hearts of the sons of men are full of evil; madness is in their hearts while they live…" (Ecc. 9:3).

Why is this?

The answer should be obvious. People do not fear the God of the Bible enough to bother keeping His commandments. Plus, in their natural unrepentant state it is difficult for them to do so anyway. "Because the carnal mind is enmity (an enemy) against God; for it is not subject to the law of God, nor indeed can be" (Rom. 8:7).

Individuals and nations want to do their own thing when they want to do it with no interference. The Apostle Paul describes the situation is these terms (Sorry, we're going to have to get involved with more Bible quotes. It's unavoidable):

"There is none righteous, no not one; There is none who understands; There is none who seeks after God. They have all turned aside; they have together become unprofitable; there is none who does good, no, not one....Their feet are swift to shed blood; destruction and misery are in their ways; And the way of peace they have not known. There is no fear of God before their eyes" (Rom. 3:10-12,15-18).

Surely you'll agree this is not a very flattering picture of mankind. But this is the way God sees us. If you fit somewhere in the above description (and the writer says you do) then you are right now in big trouble!

"Yeah, but God forgives sin and---"

Whoa, forget that. Back up a minute. That's another wavelength which at the moment we are not on. Consider this first:

In the days of Noah (back in the sixth chapter of Genesis) things weren't looking too good. The 5th verse says, "Then the Lord saw that the wickedness of man was great in the earth, and that every intent of the thoughts of his heart was only evil continually." And the 11th verse, "The earth also was corrupt before God, and the earth was filled with violence." And the 13th verse, "And God said to Noah, 'The end of all flesh has come before Me, for the earth is filled with violence through them; and behold, I will destroy them with the earth.'"

Exactly how many people were involved in this wipeout? In the fifth chapter of Genesis we have listings of men who lived for hundreds of years. One fellow named Jared lived 962 years. Another fellow named Cainan lived 910 years. And of course we have the granddaddy of them all, Methuselah, who lived 969 years. Plus many others who lived hundreds of years. These men obviously produced many children.

In the third verse of this chapter it says that Adam was 130 years old when he had a son named Seth. Then it says Adam lived another 800 years after that and had more sons and daughters. When you add this to all the children other men had who lived for many hundreds of years, it's quite possible that the earth at that time could have held a large population.

Exactly how many…we have no way of knowing. But it is not inconceivable that we might have had a couple of million people living at the time. When you have men fathering children for a period of at least 1500 years it's not that far-fetched. Who is to say that the population of the earth might not have been double or triple that number?

Yet from that vast number God found only eight people worth saving. Noah, his wife, their three sons, and their wives. Eight people out of those possible millions.

According to today's thinking that might not sound very fair. It could even be called discriminatory. But to God that did not matter. The vast majority perished in the flood-waters.

But surely there must have been in that crowd some who, by our standards, weren't so bad. No doubt there were many pregnant women who were swept away in the raging waters; there had to be thousands upon thousands of little children who were violently drowned, along with many older people who were in the nursing homes of that time.

These people enjoyed birthday parties, weddings, job advancement, and all the other things that make everyday life meaningful. Jesus said in Luke 17:26,27 that they ate and drank and married until the flood came and destroyed them all.

Evidently they were enjoying good times. There must have been many of them who were good to each other. Wedding presents were swapped, parties thrown…and yet God destroyed them because He felt they were no good.

How could He do that? Would a God to whom we cried for comfort after the World Trade Center attack, or some other natural disaster, wipe out in a violent manner children and older people just because they did not live the way He had commanded? Isn't this fanaticism? Isn't this just a bit too much?

It might be considered fanaticism if you have no (or are unaware of) righteous standards by which you are required to live. In our day and age when men do what they want because they have "rights" we create our own standards, and woe to those who interfere with them lest they find themselves on the heavy end of a lawsuit.

But God is not interested in our man-made standards or silly lawsuits. He saw that "every intent of the thoughts of men's hearts were only evil continually" (Gen. 6:5). He looked on the inside and did not like what He saw. The weddings and parties and good times and "rights" that people enjoyed at the time meant nothing to Him. Except for eight people the product was rotted beyond repair. "…everything that is on the earth shall die" (Gen. 6:17b). Destroy it and begin over.

The carnage was widespread and complete. People, animals, everything that breathed air perished under the liquid tonnage of swirling muddy waters. This was God's judgment upon sin. It was not pretty, it was not merciful, it did not wait for a ruling from some appeals court. It was final and without reprieve.

For the sake of our discussion let's use the round figure of one million people on the face of the earth at the time. Does what happened mean that 999,992 people went to Hell (or its equivalent) at that time? Eight people were saved and the rest damned not only in the flood but their souls also for all eternity?

It is almost impossible to read the situation any other way!

Does this make God seem almost too hard to deal with? It shouldn't. If God has given commandments and precepts by which He expects us to live, and we refuse, then whose fault is it when judgment falls? You would have no one to blame but yourself.

"This is crazy! You can't send the majority of people to Hell. You're interpreting it wrong."
How do you know?
"It stands to reason. A God of love would never do that."

All right, let's consider the words of Jesus in Matt. 7:13,14. "Enter by the narrow gate; for wide is the gate and broad is the way that leads to destruction, and there are many who go in by it. Because narrow is the gate and difficult (constricted) is the way which leads to life, and there are few who find it."
Or the words of Jesus in Luke 13:23,24: "Then one said to Him, 'Lord, are there few who are saved?' And He said to them, 'Strive to enter through the narrow gate, for many, I say to you, will seek to enter and will not be able."

"People will honestly seek to enter Heaven and will not be able?"
Evidently.
"But why not?"
The answer is simple: Wrong religion or wrong thinking.
"Wrong thinking…?"
Yes, you have to understand the gospel before you can apply it. It should be obvious from this verse that just being religious isn't quite enough. Throwing a buck in the collection plate, hosting the next church social, and walking in the next march for hunger or breast cancer awareness might be nice things to do, but they won't do a thing for the salvation of your soul. Did you volunteer to paint the church steeple? Fine, go ahead. But don't expect to pick up any spiritual salvation points for it.

Is God then unfair? If people are doing what they honestly feel is right, and according to their conscience, shouldn't that count for something?

And the simple answer to that is—No! God is not interested in your conscience. He is more interested in your response to the revelation He has given in the Scriptures. If He has said, "Listen, this is the way it is," then who are you to respond, "Yeah, but I don't see it that way. I think it's this way."

Due to the false teaching of some well-known Christian denominations, the value of following your conscience has been magnified far above its actual importance. They have made it a sacred duty to follow one's conscience no matter what.

But this is wrong. A man has a duty to first follow and obey the Word of God (cf. Matt. 4:4 & Ps.119:11).

Human conscience can be wrong due to being fed wrong information. Prov. 16:25 reads, "There is a way that seems right to a man, But its end is the way of death." It *seems* right because that is what this person was taught. But this wrong teaching leads to death. His conscience was a false guide.

Do you know what the word "seems" means? My dictionary says, "to appear to be true or evident." Note that it does not say it is true or evident, but rather that it "appears" to be true or evident.

When something appears to be true or evident it is because of some previous information that was ingested. You heard something, and then it was probably repeated by others you know, and since you didn't know any better, to you it was most likely true.

Unfortunately this is the way much of the world decides on right and wrong information about God and religion in general. Have you ever heard anyone say, "Well, it seems to me that God would never send anyone to Hell forever?"

If we were to base our theology on what we see in our friends and family, and on the fact that we know God loves His own creation, we might also come to that conclusion.

The average middle-class neighborhood does not seem destined for Hell. Most people we know are basically nice people. God might punish some people in the afterlife (and we must admit there are a lot of bad people around like murdering gangsters, terrorists, thieving CEOs, serial killers, lying dentists who say you need a lot of expensive dental work when you don't, etc). But to send other people to Hell forever…no, we just can't see that. A God of love would not do that.

Many people think this way, and they think this way because it is a very comfortable way to think. People like comfortable religion, and they like a comfortable God. What they do not like is the God of the Bible who is a bit tougher than the god of their basic imagination.

"Hey, wait a minute here. It seems to me---"
Hold it! No one cares what it seems to you. The Bible says there is a God in heaven with whom it is not smart to cross or mess around with. That may not sound like popular Christianity—but it's a biblical fact! This is the God who drowned possibly millions living on the earth during the great flood because they were corrupt. This is the God who destroyed the homosexuals in Sodom and Gomorrah who were so messed up they wanted to sexually abuse the angels who had come down to rescue Lot. They were all set to break down the door of Lot's house to get at them (Gen. 19:9).
"Well it still seems to me that God wouldn't kill all those people just because of their sexual orientation, along with young kids and grandparents, blah, blah…"
Oh, is that so? Well that might make a good argument on some college campus where you enjoy fiddling around with all this "diversity" rubbish, and where you can find a lot of half-baked students who enjoy sounding like experts on subjects they know nothing about, but in the real world--according to the Bible--it happened! Keep in mind that the name of this book is "If The Bible Is Really True…" and not, "If Everything We Hear On The Network News Is True."

So what "seems" is not necessarily so. And that is because divine truth is not something you can reason out. Divine truth is revelation, and revelation has to be revealed and not figured out. So what "seems" and what "is" is not necessarily the same.

This should disprove the foolishness that a man has an obligation to follow his religious conscience. Your conscience can lead you astray. Your mind and conscience can be defiled (Titus 1:15); your conscience can be seared (1 Tim. 4:2) to the point where it is "past feeling" (Eph. 4:19). It is not a reliable guide. And nowhere in the Bible are we advised to follow the dictates of our religious conscience.

The trouble with most of the world is that it hasn't the faintest idea of what God has said on the great issues affecting mans' destiny. People listen to so-called religious spokesmen, the media, public opinion, friends and relatives-- everybody but God himself.

Because of this they could be heading for big trouble.

Another concept of God (about which we hear very little) is His jealousy. "For I, the Lord your God, am a jealous God…" (Ex. 20:5). "How long, Lord? Will You be angry forever? Will your jealousy burn like fire?" (Ps. 79:5). "For the Lord your God is a consuming fire, a jealous God" (Deut. 4:24).

The God of the Bible does not want those who belong to Him following other gods or beliefs contrary to what He has revealed as best for them. Those who do follow other gods and beliefs He eventually destroys.

Listen to Moses as he recounts some of Israel's past victories over pagan societies:

"Then Sihon and all his people came out against us to fight at Jahaz. And the Lord our God delivered him over to us; so we defeated him and his sons, and all his people. We took all his cities at that time, and we utterly destroyed the men, women, and little ones of every city; we left none remaining" (Deut. 2:32-34). "And we utterly destroyed them (the kingdom of Og in Bashan) as we did to Sihon, king of Heshbon, utterly destroying the men, women, and children of every city" (Deut. 3:6).

It has been said that God's jealousy is the other side of His love. It is the zeal with which He seeks to maintain His relationship with those He loves. God's jealousy has been called the basic element in the whole Old Testament idea of God.

These people whose cities and lives had been wiped out by Israel acting as God's agent, met this fate because of their basic wickedness (Deut. 9:4). This may appear as very ruthless to some, but for the Hebrews of that time, they were told that people and objects associated with pagan cultic rites were to be regarded with abhorrence.

"And when the Lord your God delivers them (your enemies) over to you, you shall conquer them and utterly destroy them. You shall make no covenant with them nor show mercy to them. Nor shall you make marriages with them...For they will turn your sons away from following Me, to serve other gods; so the anger of the Lord will be aroused against you and destroy you suddenly" (Deut. 7:2-4).

God wants those who belong to Him to be separate and holy, and not part of the world system. In the intimate relationship of marriage, a believer could be seduced to the worship of wrong gods and ideas, exposing generation after generation to spiritual pollution. For this reason marriage was expressly forbidden with non-believers in order to guard and preserve God's covenant relationship with His people.

This same principle holds true for Christians in this present time. As the relationship was with God and the Israelite in the Old Testament, so it is with God and the Christian in the New Testament. As you cannot mix oil with water, you cannot mix truth with error, or belief with unbelief, and come out with anything for which the God of heaven can have the slightest respect. According to the Bible it just will not work!

God does not accept the biblically deficient ideas of men regardless of how noble they may sound. To believe that religion is good because it is religious, and therefore something God should be happy with, is a deadly delusion. If you have a disease, and there is only one medication that has been developed to cure that disease, taking all the other medications except that one will do you no good.

You will die.

It's the same with religion. Much of it is no good at all—and actually dangerous.

"You shall utterly destroy all the places where the nations which you shall dispossess served other gods, on the high mountains and on the hills and under every green tree. And you shall destroy their altars, break their sacred pillars, and burn their wooden images with fire; you shall cut down the carved images of their gods and destroy their names from that place. You shall not worship the Lord your God with such things" (Deut. 12:2-4).

If there were any value to pagan religions, even "some good" in them, would God have dealt so severely with them? Wouldn't He have been more inclined to say, "Well, take what's good in them and leave the rest," or something to that effect?

But He didn't do that. Instead His attitude was, "But of the cities of these peoples which the Lord your God gives you as an inheritance, you shall let nothing that breathes remain alive, but you shall utterly destroy them…lest they teach you to do according to all their abominations which they have done for their gods, and you sin against the Lord your God" (Deut. 20:16-18).

Some might incline that this principle of separation does not apply to the present day. Pagan religions were bad because they offered human sacrifices to their gods and practiced outright sexual immorality, and did other things that people of today might find horrifying.

On the surface that might sound like a reasonable argument. But remember that we are dealing with the souls of men, women and children, their ultimate destiny, and whether they end up with God in Heaven or the Devil in Hell. If the church down the street is giving out the wrong medication for the disease called sin, those ingesting it will be lost forever, and that church will be doing just as much damage as the religions in the cities the Israelites destroyed. Both, in the final analysis, do more damage than good. It's just that churches today do things in a more genteel manner. But the results, unfortunately, are still the same.

"Yeah, but that sounds bigoted. Saying that someone else's church does damage---"

Hold it, I know. This is not real American thinking. It is not the way we are used to considering things. In this country all religions have the same freedom to propagate their doctrines and beliefs, blah, blah, blah. Okay, fine. No American who believes in freedom and liberty would want it any other way.

But this does not mean that in the eyes of the Lord all these various beliefs are of equal value. Obviously they cannot be. God is not a God of mass confusion, nor is He a God who places His stamp of approval on every cockeyed religious idea that comes down the pike. God, evidently, does not subscribe to political correctness.

Some religions (and churches) are just plain wrong! And if you are in the wrong one—you could be in big trouble!

THE CHRIST OF THE BIBLE

There have been attempts by many to disassociate the Christ of the New Testament from the God of the Old Testament. In the Old Testament we supposedly find a God of wrath, while in the New Testament we find a merciful and loving Jesus.

But a careful reading of the Bible does not support this kind of thinking. If Jesus is the Son of God (or God incarnate—meaning God in the flesh) then He would have the same feelings, ideas, concepts, standards, desires, goals, attitude, etc., as the God of the Old Testament. If not, we would be dealing with a God possessing a split personality.

What many overlook is the severity of Jesus Christ when dealing with sin, hypocrites and unbelievers. All through the four gospels we find Him in bitter arguments with His religious opponents. Time after time we find Him hurling the charge of hypocrite at those whom He engaged in discussion.

"Woe to you, scribes and Pharisees, hypocrites! For you are like whitewashed tombs which indeed appear beautiful outwardly, but inside are full of dead men's bones and all uncleanness" (Matt. 23:27).

Others He called lawbreakers to their face. "Did not Moses give you the law, yet none of you keeps the law?" (John 7:19).

He told others that the Old Testament prophet Isaiah was writing of them when he said, "This people honors Me with their lips, But their heart is far from me. And in vain do they worship Me, Teaching as doctrines the commandments of men" (Mark 7:6,7).

Overall Jesus did not seem too pleased with those to whom He preached. His close followers He nurtured, but His religious opponents He scorned. At times He seemed to go out of His way to provoke them.

One particular instance took place in Luke 11:37-54. Jesus had been invited to dine at the home of a certain Pharisee. The Pharisee noticed immediately that Jesus had not washed before sitting down to eat, and evidently mentioned this.

Jesus' reaction was swift. He went right after the Pharisee telling him he was full of greed and wickedness.

This is a rough way to address someone who had just invited you to dine at his home. By today's standards it would not go over as very polite. Didn't this traveling preacher have any class, any savoir-faire? What is so bad about suggesting you might want to wash before sitting at the table?

But that was not all. In the 45th verse one of the lawyers said, "Teacher, by saying these things You reproach us also."

Judging by Jesus' response, it seems this lawyer would have been better off keeping his mouth shut, because Jesus immediately turns to him and opens up with, "Woe to you also, you lawyers!" and then proceeds to castigate him.

When I first read this I thought how interesting it would have been to be a fly on the wall and observe the reaction of those present. Here were all these noted individuals being taken over the coals by this traveling preacher whose credentials had yet to be proved. Who did He think he was talking in this manner to such important men? No doubt they thought Him very rude, someone who did not know His place, and someone who was probably very mean-spirited

But what really bothered them was the uncovering of their secret sins. When you tell people the truth about themselves they can't take it. You will hear instead that you should be more positive in your remarks, and not so negative.

But Jesus was not positive with His comments, nor did He give out constructive criticism. Instead He was very sharp and blunt with His remarks, giving no quarter, and leaving no room for excuses.

Did Jesus go about this the right way? We are constantly reminded that we should always be tactful, courteous, and of course, loving. But evidently these directives are not written in stone. It obviously depends upon the circumstances. Who you are dealing with, and the conditions of the moment, must be taken into account.

Evidently there is a time when setting forth the hard truth takes precedence over everything else. There are times when a Bible believing Christian just cannot afford to keep silent, regardless of how he might come across to others. Jesus laid out the truth without apology in a situation where He felt the hard truth was necessary.

Is this the gentle, loving Jesus we are so accustomed to reading and hearing about?

Yes and no. It is Jesus in another aspect of His ministry. It is the Jesus of the Bible who did not hesitate to tell others where to get off if He felt it was necessary. It is the true Jesus before churches felt He needed a PR man.

The severity of Jesus Christ is no different from the severity of the God of the Old Testament. God told people all throughout the Old Testament that if they did not obey His commandments they would perish.

Example: "I call heaven and earth to witness against you this day, that you will soon utterly perish from the land which you cross over the Jordan to possess; you will not prolong your days in it, but will be utterly destroyed" (Deut. 4:26).

In the thirteenth chapter of Luke, Jesus made a similar statement. Certain individuals had told Him of bad things that had happened to some Galileans (Luke 13:1-5). (Some had been killed by a falling tower, and others had their blood mingled with their sacrifices.) Jesus answered and said these individuals were no worse than others, but if the ones speaking to Him did not repent they would likewise perish.

The meaning here should be obvious. Jesus was not saying that the ones speaking to Him would have a tower fall on them, or have their blood mingled with sacrifices. He was saying that if they did not repent of their sins they would go to Hell just like the ones on whom the tower fell, and those who had their blood mingled with sacrifices.

This is hard stuff! But this is no different from what the God of the Old Testament said innumerable times. Repent or perish.

The Jesus of the New Testament was not a soft touch.

Neither was He a lighthearted, easygoing person whose main concern was healing the sick or feeding the hungry. The shortest verse in the Bible is the one that says, "Jesus wept" (John 11:35). There is no verse of any length that says Jesus ever laughed, smiled, joked or kidded around with anyone. Isaiah said, "He was a man of sorrows and acquainted with grief" (Is. 53:3). He was never the life of the party.

It might hit you as strange that a man who had a public ministry of roughly three years never once laughed or smiled. (And if He did no one thought it important enough to record.) But what was there to laugh about? His ministry was one that said, essentially, "Repent and believe on Me or you are lost!"

Talk of that nature does not bring one into many humorous situations. Talk of that nature causes friction and trouble.

In Matt. 10:34-36 Jesus said, "Do not think that I came to bring peace on earth. I did not come to bring peace, but a sword. For I have come to set a man against his father, a daughter against her mother, and a daughter-in-law against her mother-in-law, and a man's enemies will be those of his own household." And in Luke 12:51, regarding the same subject matter, Jesus said He came to bring division.

Jesus was more of a troublemaker than He was a peacemaker. The idea that He came solely to teach men to live in peace and love one another does not hold up.

He claimed that He was the Son of God, that in Him was life eternal, that He was the only way to God, and that apart from Him you were only fit to be gathered up and burned (cf. John 15:6).

There were many who did not appreciate that kind of talk.

So they killed Him.

There are many today who do not appreciate that kind of talk—so they ignore Him and ridicule His followers.

But what if what He said was true? "If you don't go along with me you are only fit to be thrown into the fire and burned?"

That's hard stuff. And so uncompromising. You can't get away with saying things like that. And how about "I am the way, the truth, and the life. No one comes to the father except through Me?" (John 14:6)

That's another tough one, so brutally uncompromising, just as rigid, and leaving no room for the good things found in other religions. Just who did this Jesus think He was…God?

Well, yes, that's exactly who He thought He was. And He never indicated that there was good in other religions, just as the God of the Old Testament never indicated there was good in the religions of other nations that came into contact with His people.

The fact that Jesus claimed to be God cannot be disputed. The gospel of John was written mainly to prove that very point. The deity of Christ literally explodes from every chapter in that book.

In Col. 1:15-18 it says (referring to Christ), that all things in heaven and earth were created by Him, and that in Him all things consist.

But wait a minute. In Gen. 1:1 it says that God created the heavens and the earth. Does the writer of the book of Colossians then contradict the writer of the book of Genesis…or are they writing about the same person under two different names?

Obviously the latter is true. To understand this any other way would make no sense. Jesus Christ is the God of the Old Testament who created the universe. He existed before Abraham (John 8:58), and that did not go over too good with those who heard this; and His goings forth have been from everlasting--or more literally—from the days of eternity (Micah 5:2).

The most perfect picture of the preexistent Christ can be found in Prov. 8:22-36. This is an adumbration (or a vague foreshadowing) of His work and presence at the beginning of creation under the name of Wisdom.

"I have been established from everlasting, From the beginning, before there was ever an earth" (vs. 23).

Who could that be? It can't be God, as He is spoken of as someone else in vs. 22. So it is someone with God. Someone who thinks and speaks. Someone who existed before God made even the primal dust of the world (vs. 26).

This person was beside God as a "master craftsman" (vs. 30) who took part in what was being created.

Then in vss. 32-36 He becomes very serious, sounding much like Jesus in the gospel of John when He was trying to establish His credentials with His detractors. Who else could say, "For blessed are those who keep my ways" (vs.32), and "For whoever finds me finds life" (vs. 35).

And most incredible of all, "All those who hate me love death' (vs. 36b).

Isn't all this very close to what Jesus said when speaking to the Jews in John 8:24? "Therefore I said to you that you will die in your sins; for if you do not believe that I am He, you will die in your sins."

If you do not believe in the Jesus of the Bible you will die forever; you will have no hope and no future. To take this position is the equivalent of loving death.

If the Bible is really true, we are dealing here with a very unique individual. One who is not pressured or pushed around. One who sets up standards and expects you to conform—or else!

We are dealing here with God in the flesh!

But for some reason most people don't seem to care. Jesus is at best an afterthought, a semi-respected religious leader, a model for those who desire to live right; and also a personage who, if we allow Him too close, or take Him too seriously, can spoil some good times.

So the world keeps Him at arms length.

It does this in a variety of ways. One of the most obvious is the way Jesus is regarded at Christmas. Have you ever noticed that Jesus Christ is one of the few (if not the only one) who, at the time of His birthday, is always depicted as a baby? When we celebrate the birthdays of other well-known men we always consider them during the moments of their greatest glory. Example:

When we remember the birthday of Martin Luther King, Jr., we immediately think of (or are shown) scenes of him delivering his famous "I have a dream…" speech.

If we were to consider the birthday of John F. Kennedy we might think of his "Ask not what your country can do for you, but what you can do for your country" speech.

On Abe Lincoln's birthday we might think of his Gettysburg Address, or of old Abe sitting in his chair in the Lincoln Memorial.

On George Washington's birthday we might think of the famous picture of him crossing the Delaware River, or huddling with his troops at Valley Forge.

One thing we do not think about, or are shown, are scenes of these men when they were babies. These men were famous people who accomplished and said certain things by which we know them. They made identifying statements.

But when we come to the birthday of Jesus Christ we are presented with scenes of a baby lying in a manger, who at that time was not capable of doing or saying anything. He has been effectively censored!

The world is comfortable with this presentation, as babies who cannot act or speak are no threat to anyone. Look at your average Christmas card and you will rarely, if ever, see Jesus Christ quoted. Most people haven't the faintest idea of anything He ever said except maybe "Love your neighbor." I am still waiting to see the first Christmas card that says: Greetings on the birthday of our Lord and Savior who said, "Therefore I said to you that you will die in your sins; for if you do not believe that I am He you will die in your sins" (John 8:24).

I have never seen anything like that and really don't expect to. It might be thought a bit divisive, or maybe not in tune with the holiday spirit--or maybe even anti-Semitic. And besides, who wants to hear anything so depressing during the Christmas season?

Unfortunately most churches have gone right along with this Christmas presentation of Jesus Christ, and in the process have theologically emasculated Him. King, Kennedy, Washington, and Lincoln were men who said important things.

Jesus Christ was a baby who said nothing.

But the Jesus of the Bible said plenty, and some of His comments were among the most profound sayings ever uttered. Who else could say, "I am the resurrection and the life…And whoever lives and believes in Me shall never die" (John 11:25,26)?

Who else could say, "He who rejects me, and does not receive My words, has that which judges him—the word that I have spoken will judge him in the last day" (John 12:48)?

You do not consider lightly one who makes such statements. You cannot afford to pass Him off as irrelevant. You cannot conclude--without prior investigation--that His ideas and opinions have nothing to do with your life, lifestyle, and final destination.

You just cannot afford to take that chance!

THE LAW OF THE BIBLE

The Bible is--among other thing--a book of rules and laws. It contains commandments, precepts, standards of conduct, etc. Many of these rules and laws run counter to what most people want to do with their time and money. Most of us have seen the bumper sticker or sign over someone's desk that reads, "Everything I like is either illegal, immoral or fattening."

That sentiment is not too far off. Sin can be very satisfying. Not to the soul, but to the immediate senses. There could be a great momentary satisfaction in killing someone you really hate; there can be great satisfaction in stealing something you really want or feel you should have; there can be great satisfaction in pulling a fast one on someone and getting away with it to your benefit.

There is momentary satisfaction in illicit sex. There is satisfaction in acquiring wealth even if others might suffer for your gain. There is satisfaction (for some) in getting so plastered and drunk that you forget all your troubles and just sit there giggling and drooling all over yourself.

Sin can satisfy the senses—but it kills the soul!

The most familiar religious laws are the Ten Commandments. They were given to Moses on Mt. Sinai about three months after he had led the children of Israel out of their Egyptian bondage (Ex. 20:1-17).

The first four commandments deal with mans' relationship to God. The fifth commandment deals with our relationship with our parents, and the last five deal with our relationship with other people.

Intentional or not, these commandments are in good order. The first thing people should concern themselves with is their relationship with God, then their families, and then their neighbors. However, in our dysfunctional society we seem to have gotten things backwards. Most people worry about their standing in the world first, their standing with their families second, and their standing with God last...if at all.

The first commandment says, "You shall have no other gods before Me."

Obviously it is of extreme importance to worship the right God, as this is the very first thing God asks of us. If you should worship the wrong god—or the gods of some non-Christian religion—you could be in big trouble.

"Hey, wait a minute. When it comes to those other gods, aren't people really worshipping the true God under a different name? Like Allah, or whatever...?"

Sorry, no. No more than they were worshipping the true God in Old Testament times under the names of Baal, Dagon, Molech, or Tammuz. The Israelites destroyed these gods along with those who worshipped them. They were not considered stand-ins for the true God.

Some have made material things their god, like wealth or personal possessions. But the moment you do this you are guilty of breaking the first commandment. And you are definitely not the man of Ps. 119:35-37, who said, "Make me walk in the path of your commandments, for I delight in it. Incline my heart to your testimonies, and not to covetousness. Turn away my eyes from looking at worthless things, and revive me in your way."

Your first obligation in all things is to God. He should be taken into account first in all that you do. Everything else comes second. This may seem difficult and maybe a "bit too much" to those not used to thinking this way; but for those who take the Bible seriously it constitutes a natural lifestyle and allows the free flow of God's blessings that nurture intimate fellowship with Him.

The second commandment says, "You shall not make for yourself a carved image of anything in heaven above, or on the earth, or in the water. You shall not bow down to them…For I the Lord your God am a jealous God…." (cf. Ex. 20: 4,5).

This commandment is obviously a prohibition against idolatry, the worship of the work of a man's hands. You will not see statues in Jewish synagogues or the great majority of Protestant churches. Unfortunately we do find them in Roman Catholic churches. This is wrong and against the second commandment.

The Catholic Church defends the use of statues by claiming that Catholics do not pray to the actual statue. The statue is only a reminder of someone else.

But that is beside the point. The commandment says do not make them—for whatever reason. The prohibition is because men would have a tendency to eventually worship what they made.

But even then they would be worshipping the power behind the piece of rock or wood, and not the object itself. In that sense the final conclusion of the matter would be no different from that reached in Catholic belief. Do not make them because you can eventually end up worshipping the powers behind them. And those powers are not God, which means you are again breaking the very first commandment.

The third commandment says, "You should not take the name of your God in vain…"

That includes "God d… it" and the name "Jesus Christ." and other references where one or a combination is used in less than a respectful or properly religious manner.

The reason for this should be evident. God is holy. He is above and separate from us. To take His name in an idle, frivolous, blasphemous, or insincere manner is demeaning to Him, places Him on our level (actually below our level), and shows that we lack the proper fear and reverence for who He is.

Consider this: Have you ever heard anyone bang his thumb with a hammer and yell out, "George Washington, that hurt?" Or when chewing out someone yell, "Moses, can't you do anything right?" Or yell, "Shakespeare" when they become upset or frustrated.

Most likely you haven't. It's always the Lord's name that is used. This is a stupid and self-conscious habit that unknowingly attempts to dethrone God, make Him of less importance, and shows (unconsciously) for Him your complete contempt.

Look at it this way. Suppose your name was Joe Smith. You liked your name and were proud of it. Then it comes to your attention that every time someone feels like yelling or screaming about something, they prefix their remarks by yelling out your name in a very derogatory manner. It wouldn't be too long before this got under your skin. You'd begin thinking that people were dumping all over you.

And you would be right!

Do you know someone who swears and curses, and in the process uses the name of Jesus Christ in an improper manner? He could be in big trouble, because concerning this, God has said, "The Lord will not hold him guiltless who takes His name in vain" (Ex. 20:7).

The fourth commandment is, "Remember the Sabbath day, to keep it holy."

The Sabbath is primarily a day of rest. Originally it had nothing to do with attending church or observing religious customs. It wasn't until much later that it became known as a day of worship

Keeping something holy means keeping it separate and apart from the usual. On an ordinary day people work. On the Sabbath they don't.

In the United States and other western countries the Sabbath has been profaned beyond belief. There is nothing sacred left to the day. All kinds of unnecessary work is performed for the sake of the almighty dollar. Stores are open from early in the morning until late at night, oftentimes with no concern for the employee's religious practices. There is no thought of keeping one day of seven separate and holy for the sake of people so they may rest and consider spiritual matters.

In any advanced society it is necessary for certain work to be performed on the Sabbath. We cannot have all policemen and firemen off duty on Sunday; we cannot have the cooks in nursing homes off on Sunday, etc. These workers must take their day of rest on another day. No one quarrels with this.

But the overall drift has been work as usual if it is profitable. This is what profanes the seventh day that the Lord blessed and hallowed.

The French thinker Voltaire is credited with saying, "If we want to destroy the Christian religion (which he actually wanted to do) we must destroy the Christian Sabbath."

The anti-Christian regime set up in France during the French Revolution attempted that very thing. They tried to destroy the Christian Sabbath in a campaign to wipe out both the Christian faith and the society upon which it rested. Some even attempted to manufacture a ten-day week in order to celebrate the mathematical genius of mankind, and totally wipe out the original Sabbath as a commemoration of the original creation.

The main reason for the Sabbath is to celebrate the work of God in creation. It was meant to be the first holiday, and was given as a day of rest for mankind. God rested on the seventh day. Man honors what God did by resting on the seventh day.

Those who mock, or attempt to destroy that cycle for the sake of personal gain, could some day find themselves in big trouble.

The fifth commandment is: "Honor your father and mother."

The family is the basic unit of society. Therefore, a strong and well-disciplined family is the bedrock of a strong and healthy society. A family cannot be disciplined if no one is in charge. Parents who do not take complete charge of their children will raise children who will not take charge of their children.

We see stark evidence of this in present-day America. Young children run wild with guns in schools, killing one another, hating those who do not conform to their standards, and ignoring parents who no doubt ignored their parents.

To honor one's father and mother is to place a restraint upon oneself. All children need restraint that consists of proper training in both family and social contact. Without it they can become a law unto themselves, eventually killing, pillaging, and destroying others and one another.

Parents normally want what is good for their children. They have "been there" and know what life is all about. Their advice is usually sound. When God tells us to honor our father and mother He is telling us to obey and learn from them so we will know how to function in the world they brought us into.

You honor your parents when you do what they say, and you honor them when you care for them when they are no longer able to care for you or themselves. Anything less than that makes you a destroyer of the basic family unit set up by God for the well-being of all mankind.

The sixth commandment is, "You shall not murder."

This is the first commandment concerning our relationship with others, and of course one of the most important.

There is no greater crime or sin than taking the life of another person. But that does not necessarily mean that all killing is wrong. Killing and murder are two different things. When a policeman shoots and kills a fleeing bank robber he is not murdering anyone; when a soldier shoots an enemy soldier he is not murdering anyone. If you shot someone who was breaking into your home to rob and possibly kill someone, you would not be murdering anyone. When the state executes a criminal it is not murdering the criminal.

These people are being killed, and not murdered, and the Bible makes a clear distinction between the two. The Bible justifies the killing of certain people in particular circumstances—and the Bible also supports the concept of capital punishment. The idea that only God has the right to take human life is just not true! This idea is usually parroted by those who have never read a Bible, but who are always quick to give God's views on the issues.

God considers the life of a man sacred. So sacred that it is not to be unjustifiably taken by another.

After the Great Flood, when God wiped out an evil generation and gave man a new start through Noah, God renewed His command of putting man in charge of everything on earth. Speaking to Noah and his family, God said, "And the fear of you and the dread of you shall be on every beast of the earth, on every bird of the air, on all that move on the earth, and on all the fish of the sea. They are given into your hand…Surely for your lifeblood I will demand a reckoning; from the hand of every beast I will require it, and from the hand of man. From the hand of every man's brother I will require the life of man. Whoever sheds man's blood, By man his blood shall be shed; For in the image of God He made man" (Gen. 9:2,5,6).

The power to kill is the supreme power of temporal rule. It belongs to God and has been delegated to man. Men have been given the right to kill any animal that takes a human life, whether it is shark, tiger, dog, or whatever. And he has also been given the right to kill any man who unlawfully takes the life of another man.

Mans' dominion over the earth is secure only as long as he has the ability to exercise the power of death to avenge crimes against his own person. To allow those who kill the right to live challenges that dominion and weakens the social fabric. God said, "You shall not pollute the land where you are; for blood defiles the land, and no atonement can be made for the land, for the blood that is shed on it, except by the blood of him who shed it" (Num. 35:32).

Such is the value of mans' life. And such is the penalty for those who unlawfully take that life, for in the eyes of God that life is beyond price.

"Moreover you shall take no ransom for the life of a murderer who is guilty of death, but he shall surely be put to death" (Num. 35:31).

The seventh commandment. "You shall not commit adultery."

Adultery does not include all sex outside of marriage (although the Bible does teach that all sexual intercourse outside of marriage is wrong and sinful). Adultery is the breaking of the marriage bond between a husband and wife, and a complete disregard for the vow made before God and man to remain faithful to one's spouse.

Adultery can happen for a number of reasons (although all are without excuse). The most common reason is that the person committing the act no longer loves or respects his/her spouse. Instead of watching out for temptation the adulterer goes looking for it. Why not get away with what you can if no one is ever going to know? Besides, since your marriage hasn't worked out the way you envisioned you have every right—or so you tell yourself.

But the Bible does not share your rationalization. The mystery of making or keeping a pledge of loyalty to God or to a spouse, the taking of the name of God in a solemn oath, these are the things upon which the moral law is built. They are the foundations of a society. Promises, vows, pledges, loyalties all vanish if they are broken with impunity. Society works only by keeping pledges and punishing violations. The bond of loyalty lies in what we might call "the spirit world." It has no shape or weight or size, nor can it be touched or seen. Yet it controls all life and associations.

Adultery is listed in the Bible right up there with the sins of fornication, idolatry, homosexuality, stealing, extortion and drunkenness. Of each sin it is said, "They will not inherit the kingdom of God" (cf. 1 Cor. 6:9,10).

The adulterer not only weakens his society, damages his family, and endangers his soul, but he is also guilty of severe emotional damage to his spouse. When the innocent party is deceived in this manner he/she is subjected to a cruelty almost impossible to define. You are first filled with self-loathing because this has happened to you, then anger, then briefly hate, and then an inner pain that fastens itself inside your very bones, of which you cannot rid yourself.

Simply put, you suffer! You want to literally kill someone, but you can't; you want to scream to the world about this horrible injustice that has happened to you, and at the same time hide in a corner alone because of the shame that you must keep secretly within you. You are wrenched first one way, and then the other, and there is no friend who can give you relief. This is one instance in which you must suffer alone. You have been deceived in a way you never imagined, and you will never again look at the world and relationships in the same light.

God has established the family as the basic unit of society. Anything that damages the family damages God's overall plan for mankind. Therefore: You shall not commit adultery!

The eighth commandment is, "You shall not steal."

I know a man who, because of his disillusionment with what is going on in America at the present time, the corruption and theft in high places, the frauds, the cons, the swindles, the fleecing of America, etc., said, "If I weren't a churchgoing man my motto would be 'Steal or be stolen from.' It's that bad."

Small-timers steal with guns; big-timers steal with pencils and with the help of their lawyers. Minimum wage employees steal from the shop; Wall St. tycoons steal from each other and the American public. Politicians steal by granting favors to those who pay off, and big business steals by contributing to politicians who give their businesses tax breaks that the average American would never be granted.

Some poor people cheat the welfare system; big corporations demand all kinds of tax breaks or threaten to move their companies elsewhere (corporate welfare) and in the process cheat the American public who are forced to make up the difference. Ours is a society that functions on thievery. But this would not happen without the consent of the individual, acting alone or as part of the group.

This commandment is part of what we know as the natural rights of man. The founding fathers of the United States divined that all free men had the right to life, liberty, and property. But all three of these rights can be stolen from them. A man can be murdered, he can be unjustly imprisoned, he can be forced to give up all his belongings. He can, in a word, be stripped of his manhood and livelihood and become no better than an animal who expects no other right than to live and eat, whether this be in a jail cell or a cold water shack.

When you steal, whether you use a gun or a pencil, or if your hands work in secret, you defy the God of heaven whose "eyes are in every place, keeping watch on the evil and the good" (cf. Prov. 15:3).

The ninth commandment, "You shall not bear false witness against your neighbor" is a clear injunction against lying.

The Bible is filled with warnings against the sin of lying. It says, "Lying lips are an abomination to the Lord, But those who deal truthfully are His delight" (Prov. 12:22).

Lying should not be considered a minor sin. In Hosea 4:1,2 God says, concerning the land of Israel, "There is no truth or mercy or knowledge of God in the land. By swearing and lying, killing and stealing and committing adultery, they break all restraint, with bloodshed upon bloodshed."

Lying is listed right up there along with some of the worst things you can do. Lying is also the most frequently committed sin. It is committed openly and flagrantly in courtrooms all over America every day in the week, even after a person has sworn to tell the truth, the whole truth, and nothing but the truth—so help them God.

The O.J. Simpson trial saw wholesale lying on a grand scale by the defense, the prosecution witnesses, witnesses for the defense, lawyers, and even those who were not part of the trial but who made self-serving statements in order to further their own celebrity and chance to make money from the misfortune of others. No one cared for the truth. The only thought was that of winning. Winners make more money than losers.

Lying is endemic in our society. Doctors and hospitals lie when filling out health insurance forms; politicians lie if they feel it will further their political careers; dentists lie by claiming you have three cavities, when you really have only one; car salesman lie when they tell you about the condition or past history of a used car; people lie on their income tax forms; lawyers lie and oftentimes swindle their own clients to make additional money; the government lies when it tells you it's going to do something about a particular problem, and then conveniently forgets about it after the votes are in.

Bearing false witness against your neighbor also means that you have no right to falsely accuse him. The law holds every witness accountable. If it did not, courtrooms would be even more chaotic.

It is necessary to severely punish any witness who lies, and this is done by charging them with perjury, for which there is due penalty.

In the Bible false witnesses are dealt with severely. Deut. 19:18-21 reads: "And the judges shall make careful inquiry, and if indeed the witness is a false witness, who has testified falsely against his brother, then you shall do to him as he thought to have done to his brother; so shall you put away the evil from among you. And those who remain shall hear and fear, and hereafter they shall not again commit such evil among you. Your eye shall not pity; life shall be for life, eye for eye, tooth for tooth, hand for hand, foot for foot."

The comment that "Your eye shall not pity" is an interesting point. We do not ordinarily think of God and those who believe in Him as ones who do not pity the poor, the unfortunate, or those who might be guilty of the most horrible crimes. Pity and compassion usually go hand in hand, because it is understood that "there but for the grace of God go I," and who would not want to be thought of in a compassionate manner if he were in big trouble with the law?

Yet here and in other parts of the Bible, (vss. 11-13) the idea of pitying those who flagrantly violate the law of God is unknown.

But keep in mind that we are dealing here not with personal relationships, but rather with the functioning of a stable society. You and I can forgive and show mercy, but the state, representing everyone, cannot.

When Fred Goldman told O.J. Simpson that if he would confess to killing Goldman's son, then he would drop the charges against him and refuse the money he had won in the civil trial—he had every right to do that.

But the state could not do that. The law has to take its proper course. If it did not it would corrupt itself into meaninglessness. The law, when functioning properly, shows no mercy. It does not pity. It exacts a penalty.

The purpose of the law is to punish those who violate its precepts. Punishment is supposed to teach those who have not yet violated the law that this is what can happen to them if they should violate it. This may sound like a very elementary presentation of something we usually consider quite technical in its depth, but it is the very bedrock of any legitimate legal system.

Punishment, by its very nature, is meant to be a deterrent to crime. The Bible says, "And those who remain shall hear and fear, and hereafter they shall not commit such evil..." (Deut. 19:20).

The same principle carries over into the New Testament church. The Apostle Paul says, concerning church leaders,

"Those who are sinning rebuke in the presence of all, that the rest also may fear" (1 Tim. 5:20).

"Hey, wait a minute. What kind of life is that, always walking around being afraid? This sounds like the old KGB in communist Russia, always spying on people."

No one is advocating any spying. The point here is that you are supposed to fear God if you are sinning.

"Yeah, well God doesn't want people to fear Him."

Are you sure of that...? Perhaps you should try reading the Bible a bit more carefully.

This whole question is a matter of showing God and His law the respect they deserve. The Bible demands this. When others receive punishment for their crimes you are expected to learn from their experience and avoid the same actions. If you do not, then don't expect the law to be merciful. It's that simple.

The tenth commandment: "You shall not covet your neighbor's house; you shall not covet your neighbor's wife, nor his male servant, nor his female servant, nor his ox, nor his donkey, nor anything that is your neighbor's"...could use some clarifying.

This commandment does not say it is wrong to want things that might be just as good as your neighbors. It does not say it is wrong to keep up with the Smiths. What it does say is that it is wrong to covet the particular thing your neighbor owns. If your neighbor buys a brand new Cadillac and you say to yourself, "Boy, I'd like to own a car like that," that's fine. Get a better job, save your pennies, whatever...and maybe you can buy one too.

The problem is in wanting (coveting) the actual Cadillac that is now sitting in your neighbor's driveway. That is his car, and you have no right to it—and you are wrong in coveting it.

If a fellow you know marries a very beautiful girl, and you attend the wedding and think to yourself, "Boy, would I like a wife like her," that's all right. But if your thinking runs to, "Boy, would I like to have her to be my wife," then we have a problem. You are now coveting your neighbor's wife, and that's a no-no.

Coveting breeds temptation. In the epistle of James it says, "But each one is tempted when he is drawn away by his own desires and enticed. Then, when desire has conceived, it brings forth sin; and sin, when it is full-grown, brings forth death" (James 1:14,15).

Coveting may seem somewhat harmless on the surface, but it can fester in a man's soul, then soil his mind, and eventually cause him to commit actions he would not have otherwise.

WAS (IS) JESUS REALLY GOD?

By all worldly standards, Jesus was not God. When we consider what we know (or think) about someone like God, and then consider Jesus Christ, there is no comparison.

Jesus was never a king, prime minister, or president of anything. In fact He did not even have a high-class job. He was not a world traveler, and never claimed to know much of what was going on outside His own country. The rulers of other nations knew little about Him, and He was not considered important enough to inquire after (except by the immediate Roman authorities).

Not only did other nations swear Him no allegiance, He was even rejected by His own people. His followers were few, and at the time of His arrest even they deserted Him. His public ministry was about three years in length, and at its completion there was nothing built in His name, no honors given, no memorial erected. He did not even have His own burial plot, but had to be buried in someone else's tomb.

He ended up being executed like a common criminal after the religious people of the time kept yelling, "Crucify him, crucify him!"

Surely if God were going to take on human form He would want to be portrayed by someone with more stature, bearing, and public acclaim, than this insignificant failure named Jesus.

Any way you look at it, this Jesus, measured by ordinary standards, was most likely not the God of the universe, the creator of all things, the almighty God of the Old Testament, the Alpha and Omega, the beginning and the end of all things, the One who existed before time began....

Unless you look at it through the pages of your Bible!

To read the New Testament, and come away with the belief that Jesus Christ was not divine, that He was not one with the Father, or simply put—that He was not God in the flesh—is an intellectual impossibility. The evidence of His divinity is overwhelming.

Consider this: In the four gospels (Matthew, Mark, Luke and John), Jesus performed works of which no human being is capable. He restored sight to the blind with only a word, healed others of physical afflictions using no medication of any kind, fed thousands with only a few loaves of bread and a few fish, and raised a man from the dead who had been entombed for four days.

The man raised from the dead was named Lazarus, and his story can be found in John 11:1-44. This one incident by itself should be enough to settle for all time the question of whether or not Jesus was actually God in the flesh, because how can you raise someone from the dead who had been dead for four days and most likely beginning to decay...and do it just by saying, "Lazarus, come forth?"

This was not some magician's stunt. It was not a David Copperfield illusion. Lazarus died and was buried while Jesus was somewhere else. Jesus had no part in the burial or its preparation. When He heard that Lazarus was dead He told His followers beforehand that He was going to raise him from the dead (vs. 11-14).

Visualize the setting. Jesus comes and is told that Lazarus has already been dead four days; but Jesus, with the sisters of Lazarus, comes to the tomb anyway. He says, "Take away the stone." (Lazarus had been buried in a cave and a huge stone had been placed against the entrance.)

Immediately everyone gets a bit shook, especially one of the sisters who says, "Lord, by this time there is a stench, for he has been dead four days."

This sister, Martha, at the time still did not fully understand the whole picture. People rarely did when Jesus spoke. He would talk "beyond" them at times, in parables at other times, and sometimes answer them so indirectly that they would miss His full meaning. He did not tell Martha and Mary directly that He was going to raise their brother from the dead…but all the implications where there. He said in vs. 23, "Your brother will rise again." But Martha did not believe that He meant immediately. She thought that He was speaking about the Last Day.

Did Jesus then stop to correct her misconception? No, He did not. He spoke "beyond" her and proceeded to make one of the most amazing statements recorded in the Bible when He said, "I am the resurrection and the life. He who believes in Me, though he may die, he shall live. And whoever lives and believes in Me shall never die…." (vs. 25,26).

Who speaks like this without being outright insane—or God himself? Who dares make such a statement in public? When someone talks like this he had better be able to back it up, or immediately lose all credibility about anything.

Martha's answer to Jesus' statement still gave no indication that she knew exactly what He was talking about. It was momentarily beyond her.

So they took away the stone. The crowd is watching. No doubt most of them expected Jesus to view the corpse and then have the stone rolled back into place.

But instead Jesus lifts His eyes and begins to pray aloud. And then came the words, "Lazarus, come forth!"

All eyes turn toward the cave. Nothing is happening. Then someone cried out, "Look!"

In the darkness of the cave something was moving. It moved slowly toward the cave's entrance. And then it came out into the open, barely able to walk because of the graveclothes that restricted its movement. The body is wrapped hand and foot, and a cloth is wrapped around its face. It stops at the entrance to the cave…and the people at this point are wide-eyed.

A dead man who should be rotting by now is standing in front of them. How could this be happening? This is impossible! But the man with his rags hanging off him is still standing there, and his presence defies every explanation. In fact don't even try to explain it. Just look and try to believe your own eyes.

Imagine being there at the time. Imagine the chills that would run the entire length of your body as you watched in stunned silence.

And then Jesus said, "Loose him, and let him go."

And that is the end of the incident. The writer adds nothing more, and we are left flabbergasted, numbed beyond belief…and possibly even frightened.

Who is the one who did this? How did He do it? And what does it all mean?

You would have an immediate urge to discuss this with others. You would have to get their opinions, and share yours with them. In your circle of friends everyone would be talking fast, stating what they think, walking around the room with their hands in the air as if trying to drag an explanation from somewhere.

But there would be no other explanation, other than the one that this Jesus spoke three words, and in the process brought a dead man back to life. Only God could do that.

Live with it!

One of the most powerful arguments for the deity of Jesus Christ can be found in the Gospel of John, the first three verses. It reads:

"In the beginning was the Word, and the Word was with God, and the Word was God.

"He was in the beginning with God.

"All things were made through Him, and without Him nothing was made that was made."

The writer is telling us that the Word (obviously Jesus as is plain from the context, cf. vs. 14) existed in the very beginning. He then goes on to tell us that this Word (Jesus) was with God and also was God himself.

But how can one be with God, and at the same time be God also? Could you possibly be standing on the corner with Harry, and at the same time also be Harry? It doesn't make sense, unless…

There is obviously more than one person in the Godhead. There are three: Father, Son, and Holy Spirit, and they are called The Blessed Trinity. It is not our immediate purpose to attempt an explanation of this, but only to say for the moment that we see in these verses two of the three mentioned.

The writer is telling us that God and the Word are the same. If the Word is the same as God, then the Word is God. Meaning Jesus is God.

He was in the very beginning with God. And what did God do in the very beginning? "In the beginning God created the heavens and the earth" (Gen. 1:1).

And what does our writer say of the Word in vs. 3 of our present text? "All things were made through Him, and without Him nothing was made that was made." In other words, the Word (Jesus) created all things.

So, if God created all things (Gen. 1:1), and without Jesus nothing was made that was made (John 1:3), then Jesus and God are obviously one and the same.

Consider also the words of Jesus when He said, "And he who sees Me sees Him who sent Me" (John 12:45), and "I and My Father are one" (John 10:30); and in one of His heated discussions with the Jews, He said, "Most assuredly, I say to you, before Abraham was, I AM" (John 8:58). This last reference means, of course, that He existed before Abraham, which could not be unless He were God himself.

(Yes, angels also existed before Abraham, but there is nothing in the Bible to suggest that Jesus was some kind of super-angel. The evidence leans overwhelmingly in the other direction.)

There was no mistaking the claims of Jesus. His antagonists at the time understood fully what He meant. In John 5:18 it is written, "Therefore the Jews sought all the more to kill Him, because He not only broke the Sabbath, but also said that God was His father, making himself equal with God."

The honest inquirer cannot escape the fact that the Bible very clearly teaches that Jesus was (is) God in the flesh. The Apostle Peter said it plainly when he wrote, "To those who have obtained like precious faith with us by the righteousness of our God and Savior Jesus Christ" (2 Pet. 1:1).

Can you refer to Jesus as God any plainer than that?

Can you say that Jesus is the God of Gen. 1:1 any plainer than the Apostle Paul when he wrote of Jesus, "For by Him all things were created that are in heaven and that are on earth, visible and invisible…" (Col. 1:16)?

No, you cannot.

Live with it!

JESUS AND HELL

It will surprise many that Jesus said more about people going to Hell than any other person in the Bible. That is not a very comforting thought, as we usually associate Him with forgiving sin, telling the woman caught in adultery that she should go and sin no more, and being a very tender and compassionate person.

And it can be said that He is. We cannot question the love that Jesus has for mankind. If that love did not exist there would be no cross, and then of course no salvation. There would be (assuming the Bible is true) no hope for the future, no eternal life, no heaven where we could rejoice with loved ones forever more in the presence of God.

You would be no better off than a dead cat.

And yet Jesus spoke many times of people being cast into a furnace of fire where there would be "wailing and gnashing of teeth" (Matt. 13:42).

Have you ever gnashed your teeth? To gnash your teeth is to grind them together, and one does not do that unless he is in severe pain. Combine that with wailing (in other places the word used is "weeping") and you have a very miserable condition. And when you consider that this situation is going to last forever, time without end, we have a condition that should be avoided at all cost.

Yet for some insane reason we have people who could care less, and among them are many who claim to accept the Bible as divine truth.

Hell is almost impossible for the human mind to fully comprehend. When you hear someone say in a cavalier manner, "Well if I go to Hell all my friends will be there," it betrays a total lack of understanding. Are your friends somehow going to make Hell more livable? Will their presence do something for you? Will you have a better time there because you'll be with people you know? Do you think that if you get everybody together you might be able to improve things by throwing a party and sending out for pizza?

Forget it. Your friends will be weeping and gnashing their teeth just like you. You might have a tough time seeing them anyway, as Hell has also been described as a place of "outer darkness" (Matt. 8:12). So instead of a place where you and your friends will get together for a good time in the afterlife (even if the place is kind of lousy), visualize instead voices screaming in the darkness, and pain from the dark fires of Hell so intense that you're screaming and grinding your teeth in pain.

And last, but far from least, keep in mind that this lasts forever!

This is not a very pretty picture, nor is it a future that any sane person would want. But sin, being what it is, deceives and slays its millions, and will most likely fill Hell with a standing room only crowd.

The question immediately arises, "How could a loving God send people to a place like that?"

The sensible reply is, "How could anyone, being warned that there might be a place like that, be so stupid that he doesn't do everything he can to make sure he doesn't end up there?"

But we are getting ahead of ourselves. What did Jesus say about all this?

First of all, He made it very clear that Hell is not hard to come by. In Matt. 5:22 He said, "Whoever says, 'You fool!" shall be in danger of Hell fire."

No one goes to Hell because he called someone else a fool. But--the attitude that would evoke this comment is one that could lead to further aggressiveness and sin. Notice that Jesus did not say you are going to Hell because of these words. He only said you would be in "danger" of Hell fire because of these words. Your attitude toward others has opened the door that could easily lead to disaster.

In Matt. 8:12 Jesus speaks of those who would be cast into outer darkness where there would be weeping and gnashing of teeth. These were the "sons of the kingdom," the Jews, His chosen ones. They would be swept into Hell because of their lack of belief in Him. (See the full context, vs. 5-13.)

One of Jesus' most telling statements is found in Matt.10:28 where he said, "And do not fear those who kill the body but cannot kill the soul. But rather fear Him who is able to destroy both soul and body in Hell."

In other words, watch your step, pal. The death of the body is nothing compared to the death of ones' soul. Men may kill you and end your temporal life—but God can go one step further. He can destroy your soul in Hell. Therefore He is the one you should really fear, and not just the guy with the gun.

God can destroy your soul in Hell…?

If the Bible is really true this is a fact you cannot escape. Yet in everyday religious discussion this fact is rarely mentioned. We do not like to think of a God who would do such things. It makes us uneasy, a little less independent. But if you're going to realistically consider the God of the Bible then you must consider Him in this manner. Like it or not, God sends the souls and bodies of men to Hell where they will suffer forever.

In Matt. 23:15 Jesus lit into the Pharisees when He said, "Woe to you, scribes and Pharisees, hypocrites! For you travel land and sea to win one proselyte, and when he is won, you make him twice as much a son of Hell as yourselves."

Obviously Jesus did not think much of the Pharisees. If He called them sons of Hell then He must have thought they were heading in that direction. They were religious phonies, two-faced fakers, hypocritical con men who considered only outward appearances, unaware that the attitude of their heart was out of joint. Jesus went even further in verse 33 when He said, "Serpents, brood of vipers. How can you escape the condemnation of Hell?"

Let's keep in mind here that Jesus is speaking to some of the upstanding citizens of the day. These men were looked up to, honored in religious circles, respected when they spoke. Yet Jesus saw that they would have trouble escaping the damnation of Hell.

Did He know something that others of that time did not know or consider? Evidently He did. And that is that true religion is not so much outward action as it is inner attitude. The Pharisees were the classic example of how not to operate. Self-righteous stuffed shirts in clerical garb do not necessarily have all the answers. How many times in our day do we hear of clergymen making pronouncements on issues like homosexuality, claiming that same sex marriages (or other whacko ideas) are just fine, when the very Bible they claim to preach from says very clearly, "You shall not lie with a male as with a woman. It is an abomination?" (Lev. 18:22). It happens all the time, and those who approve of these happenings do so because it all sounds so fair and politically correct, so nondiscriminatory—and because other religious and political leaders say this is only right.

In Israel many followed the thinking of the Pharisees who, Jesus said (Matt. 23:15), were leading other people into Hell along with them.

This is hard stuff. The average person does not usually think of clergymen leading anyone into Hell. Isn't it their job to do just the opposite?

Well…yeah. But evidently we cannot always count on them to do just that. The Bible makes the following very clear:

Some clergymen are losers!

Many people consider the very idea of Hell a remnant of superstition quite unsuited for the present enlightened age.

But this was not so with Jesus. For Him, Hell was a very present reality that was carried all through His teaching, and by the rest of the Bible carried all the way to the end of time.

"So it will be at the end of the age. The angels will come forth, separate the wicked from among the just, And cast them into the furnace of fire. There will be wailing and gnashing of teeth" (Matt. 13:49,50).

And John, speaking in the book of Revelation, the last book in the Bible, said, "The Devil, who deceived them, was cast into the lake of fire and brimstone where the beast and the false prophet are. And they will be tormented day and night forever and ever…And anyone not found written in the Book of Life was cast into the lake of fire" (Rev. 20:10,15).

If the Bible is really true, the lake of fire will be the final destination for a major part of the human race. (And maybe a large percentage of everyone you know.)

A careful study of the biblical uses of the words "life" and "death" will show that the root ideas are respectively "union" and "separation." Physical life is union of the spirit with the body; spiritual life is the union of the spirit with God. And everlasting life is this union perfected and consummated for all eternity.

Physical death, on the other hand, is the separation of the spirit from the body; spiritual death is the separation of the spirit from God. Eternal death is the perpetuation of this separation. Therefore for all who have not experienced the second birth ("Unless one is born again he cannot see the kingdom of God" (John 3:3), the second (eternal) death becomes inevitable.

(He who is only born once dies twice, but he who has been born again dies only once.)

When Jesus spoke about Hell, He did not weaken or gloss over its severity. Nor did He undermine its overall importance. In Mark 9:45 He said, "And if your foot causes you to sin, cut it off. It is better for you to enter life lame, rather than having two feet, to be cast into hell, into the fire that shall never be quenched."

"Hey, wait a minute. That's a little hard. In fact it's fanaticism! He can't mean that it's actually good to cut off your own foot?"

But that's exactly what He said.

"Yeah, but you're taking that too literally."

All right, let's look at it this way. You will be alive for roughly 76 years, give or take a few years either way. Seventy-six years, when matched against eternity, is barely a grain of sand compared to all the sand on all the beaches on this planet. If what Jesus said is true (and it just might be) you would be a first class idiot to not cut off your foot if doing that could prevent you from suffering the flames of Hell for all eternity.

But most people—deep in their hearts—are skeptical at best that Hell even exists. And even more doubt that God would send them there anyway. (What the heck, when compared to most people you're not so bad.) So it's comfortable to be like everyone else and not worry about it.

But Jesus never hinted that Hell was something about which we need not worry. If anything, He intimated just the opposite. He warned people constantly about this fate that was worse then death. He even said of Judas, the one who betrayed Him, that it would have been better for him if he had not even been born (Mark 14:21). Hell is obviously that bad!

But back to our friend with the sinning foot (or hand, or mouth, or genitals, or whatever…) who feels that this whole trade-off is just a bit too much. Is it really that difficult to imagine being in a position that is so bad you actually wished you had never been born? Wouldn't the unconsciousness of non-existence be preferable to the consciousness of unending torment? Can't you see Judas in Hell wishing that he had never betrayed anyone, that he had never gotten mixed up with Jesus in the first place, that he had never been born?

Jesus indicated that Hell is basically a fate worse than death. Some of us might die horrible and lingering deaths. It happens every day all over the world, in sick beds, on battlefields, in flaming crashes, in prison camps, hospitals, etc. Death can be a sudden and gruesome encounter that can hurl one unexpectedly into the unknown.

But the situation becomes even worse when one then finds himself in the flames of Hell with those who are weeping and gnashing their teeth; in a Hell where the door behind them has been slammed shut and bolted, locked forever with mighty chains that cannot be broken. A Hell from which there is no escape. A Hell in which the roar of the flames and the screams of the damned pound in your ears, where the heat is suffocating, where voices are cursing one another and shrieking their bitter hate at the God of the universe…forever!

It will be at that moment when a person will honestly wish that he or she had never been born.

One of the most striking illustrations Jesus used when teaching about Hell is found in Luke 16:19-31. A beggar named Lazarus, who lived a difficult life, died and was transported by the angels to Abraham's bosom (heaven), and a rich man died and was buried—and then found himself in torments in Hades (Hell). The rich man cried out for mercy, asking for water to cool his tongue for he was being tormented in the flames.

(Forget these clowns who teach that Hell is really not like this, but is only the absence of God's love or presence, or whatever. If the Bible is really true then it's obvious they don't know what they're talking about. Imagine Hitler, Joe Stalin, and some mad ax murderer sitting together someplace in the after life where there is no presence of God or expression of His love. Do you think they'd care? They most likely wouldn't want Him around anyway. If they had an interesting life killing and conquering with plenty of wine, women and song, with never a dull moment and no God in their lives to bother them, and now in the after life sitting around with still no God in the vicinity to love them or show any concern—do you really think they would consider that a bad deal? If you can commit horrible evils and then end up in a place like that, I'm sure you would find quite a few people anxious to sign up. Just think, a whole eternity to hang around doing what you want with no God always looking over your shoulder.

But the Bible does not describe a Hell of that kind. The above three men will not be sitting around talking about the good old days. Nor would they be sorrowful about the lack of God's presence. They wouldn't care! And why should they? Yet there are many simpleminded clergymen and seminary professors who continue their tired refrain that Hell is really the absence of God's love and that this is severe punishment in itself.)

But back to the rich man. He did not receive mercy or water. He received nothing. And he was reminded that there was a great gulf between him and where Lazarus was now being comforted.

This is a sobering situation, to say the least. When you are in Hell there is no mercy, no relief of any kind, and no way you can ever get out, or have anyone come to give you some kind of break. There is no parole or furlough. It's all over! The final nail, as the saying goes, has been hammered into the coffin, never to be removed.

It is the finality of Hell that that constitutes its most terrifying aspect. We don't like to think of anything being that final. We are used to changes, or the opportunity to make things change. We are used to running the show, or we are used to someone else running the show on our behalf, even if we have to pay through the nose.

But to be slammed into a place like this from which there is no reprieve, no change, no hope of escape, is something that many find incomprehensible. They will not accept this concept, or any part of it. So they deny it—to their peril!

In the 27th and 28th verses the rich man begs that Lazarus might be sent to warn his brothers about this horrible place. He doesn't want them ending up like him in this rotten place of torment.

That request is also denied. (In fact we can be reasonably sure that all requests made in Hell will be denied. This is part of what makes it Hell.) He is told that no sign will be effective with his brothers. They will have to instead pay some attention to what Moses and the prophets wrote, or to put things more simply—begin taking the Bible seriously. This is the only thing that is going to help this man's brothers.

But the rich man still argues. He is convinced that his brothers will smarten up if they hear from someone who has just come back from the dead.

But he is told, No. It just does not work that way. Those who spurn the message of God's word are not going to be convinced of God's truth by some other means.

The teaching here should be obvious. Religious miracles of any kind, no matter how well-meaning and positive they may be, cannot, of themselves, change the hearts of those momentarily influenced by them. The solid change one needs can only be brought about by the preaching of the biblical message that leads to repentance and then conversion.

What is the basic reason for one to end up in Hell? Above every other sin, it is the sin of unbelief. Consider this:

In John 8:51 Jesus said, "Most assuredly, I say to you, if anyone keeps My word he shall never see death."

"Ah…yeah, but what if I lead an exemplary life apart from all that?"

It evidently does not matter.

"But what if you don't care too much about what Jesus said and did, and yet you did a lot of good things for a lot of people? What if you were a philanthropist and helped improve society and the lives of many other people?"

It evidently does not matter.

"Well let's suppose I follow the teachings of my own religion perfectly?"

It evidently does not matter. Your religion might not be any good anyway.

Why is personal belief in Christ and His word so important? For the simple reason that belief in Him is-- according to Him--the only way to the Father. If He is wrong on this, then of course don't worry any further. Your own particular religion might do the job. After all, isn't that what religions are for?

But if He is right on this, then many people are going to be faced with a big problem. In John 10:9 Jesus said, "I am the door, if anyone enters by Me, he will be saved..." (Translated: Try getting in through any other entrance and you won't make it.)

You cannot get any more cut and dried than that. That is very tight language by any standard. Only God or a total madman would say something like that. It eliminates many very nice people who feel they can handle things their way and that God is a big god who doesn't think in such narrow terms. And of course their good life plays a big part in being accepted by God.

But this kind of reasoning eliminates the very reason for Jesus' overall ministry. He came to save people from Hell. (How often do you hear that?) But how does he save someone who does not believe in Him? How does He save someone who does not come to Him? He made that the number one prerequisite. You cannot come to the Father without going through Him first. He said that, and you had better learn to live with it—or die without it!

The Bible says, "He who believes in the Son has everlasting life; and he who does not believe the Son shall not see life, but the wrath of God abides on him" (John 3:36).

Are you a Muslim who is counting on Allah to save you...forget it! Are you a Jew who feels that because of all your people have gone through for the past 2000 years you deserve some kind of special break when you die…forget it! Are you a Roman Catholic who feels that as long as people in false religions (or any religion, including your own) are sincere and are doing their best according to their religion they'll make out…forget it! Are you an agnostic or atheist who feels none of this really makes any difference because we're all going to the same place anyway, wherever that might be…forget it!

Apart from Jesus Christ there is only one destination: Hell!

Yes, that is very tight thinking, and yes it does seem (at least according to our current standards) unfair.

If you don't like it then argue with your Bible. If it's wrong then you can give a huge sigh of relief for the many friends and family members you might have who go through life ignoring the claims of Christ.

But if all this is really true….

WHAT IS SIN?

Some years ago there was a popular song titled *What Is This Thing Called Love.* Love was supposedly something hard to figure and not the same for everyone. It hit people different ways, and some people it never hit at all.

Sin, however, is not so mysterious. A good Bible dictionary defines sin as: "lawlessness or transgression of God's will, either by omitting to do what God's law requires or by doing what it forbids. This transgression can occur in thought (I John 3:15), word (Matt. 5:22), or deed (Rom. 1:32)."

Mankind was originally created without sin. But sin entered the human experience when Adam and Eve ignored the direct command of God and ate of the forbidden fruit in the Garden of Eden.

"Whoa, wait a minute here."

All right, what do you want now?

"Are you trying to tell me that you actually believe there were two people named Adam and Eve and that all this trouble started just because they ate an apple, or whatever..."

Yes, that's exactly what I'm trying to tell you.

"But that story is a myth, a fable that has been used for the purpose of getting across some teaching, or something like that..."

How do you know that?

"Well everybody know that."

If everyone knows that then it must be very easy to prove, so let's see some evidence that this is true.

"Uhh...."

If Adam and Eve did not personally exist, then how do we know if anyone in the book of Genesis really existed? Did Cain then really kill Abel? How do we know if Noah really built an ark? Maybe the story of Joseph is a lot of baloney also. Who is to say...?

But if the Bible is really true as written, and the author had no reason to "invent stuff," then Adam and Eve really did exist as personalities, and their disobedience in the Garden of Eden was responsible for sin entering the human race.

But not everyone, whom you would think believes this, actually believes it. The latest from some Roman Catholic sources all but eliminates Adam and Eve as personal historic entities, intimating that the prototypical qualities of their names "suggests" that their story is really the story of all mankind.

But this is pure guesswork and not worthy of serious consideration. Furthermore, where does this then leave us with the doctrine of original sin? Did the masses sin somewhere along the line, or was it two individuals as the Bible clearly teaches?

Some Roman Catholic theologians have said, "God may have chosen one male and female out of a humanoid population to bear the consciousness of His image and likeness."

But why should anyone believe that, since there is no evidence of any kind that this took place? Again, it's all guesswork, and anyone who stakes the salvation of his soul on some other person's guesswork is insane!

When reading the four gospels there is no question that Jesus took the writings of the Old Testament as fully authentic just the way they were written. He understood them to be historically true. In Matt. 19:4 He said, in a direct reference to Adam and Eve, "Have you not read that He who made them at the beginning made them male and female...."

The Apostle Paul also took the story of Adam and Eve as factual. He wrote: "For Adam was formed first, then Eve. And Adam was not deceived, but the woman being deceived, fell into transgression" (1 Tim. 2:13,14).

There is nothing here about humanoids or myths; there is nothing here to suggest that Jesus did not consider the account of Adam and Eve in the book of Genesis to be historically accurate. There is nothing here to suggest that the Apostle Paul did not take the Genesis account seriously. He even wrote of Adam being one distinct person when he said, "Therefore, just as through one man sin entered the world, and death through sin, and thus death spread to all men, because all sinned—" (Rom. 5:12).

Of course there is always the chance that neither Jesus nor Paul knew what they were talking about.

But I wouldn't bet on it!

Sin originated with the Devil. He was the first sinner and this is somewhat described in both Isaiah and Ezekiel. In Ez. 28:12 the writer says, "Son of man, take up a lamentation for the king of Tyre, and say to him, 'Thus says the Lord God...'"

But what follows goes far beyond the king of Tyre, or for that matter any human being. It evolves into the description of a perfectly created angelic being who was perfect in all his ways until iniquity was found in him. Then he was cast out of the mountain of God.

He was very beautiful and very proud, and corrupted his own wisdom for the sake of his beauty (vs. 17). He became filled with violence and sinned.

A companion passage can be found in Is.14:12-15, where it is written, "How you are fallen from heaven, O Lucifer, son of the morning." And what follows is a sad commentary about a spiritual being who had it all, and because of his pride threw it all away. Look at vs.13 and you can almost weep for him. Everything is I, I, I. All he cared about (like so many people we know) was being Number One.

But he never became Number One. He never rose above God. Instead he was assigned to the lowest depths in Hell (vs.15).

You cannot knock God off His throne. Yet that is exactly what so many attempt when they live in riotous sin with no regard for the law of God. Their fate will be the same as Lucifer's. "And anyone not found written in the Book of Life was cast into the lake of fire" (Rev. 20:15).

The fact that sin is universal and affects everyone goes without saying. The great majority of reports on your TV broadcasts, or in your daily newspapers, are really reports about sin. Wars, killings, and various forms of theft and swindles are the big ones. You cannot escape them, as they are everywhere. What you think is the nightly news is many times the Nightly Sin Report.

The Cold War may be over, but now there are hot wars flaring everywhere, from the Middle East, to Africa, to the Balkans, to Iraq, possibly Korea, and who knows where next. We have even witnessed a resurgence in genocidal killings. Tribe against tribe, ethnic group against ethnic group, Muslims against Christians, and on and on it goes, never to be fully resolved.

And all because of that little three letter word S-I-N.

The writer in the book of Ecclesiastes said, "Truly the hearts of the sons of men are full of evil; madness is in their hearts while they live" (Ecc. 9:3).

That is a very accurate assessment of our present condition. In fact it has been accurate since the very beginning of the book of Genesis. The first recorded sin of man against man was murder. Cain killed Abel, his own brother. His own flesh and blood. You can't go much lower than that. It started bad in the first family and it's been like that ever since.

"And what does the Lord require of you but to do justly, to love mercy, and to walk humbly with your God?" (Micah 6:8). That doesn't sound like a very tough program. In fact if we took a poll we'd probably find a majority of votes in favor. "Wouldn't it be nice if everyone acted like that," would be the cry. "Yeah, the world would be a better place," would be another comment.

The conclusion of all life is, according to another writer, "Fear God and keep His commandments. For this is man's all" (Ecc. 12:13).

That doesn't sound so tough. In fact, since most people say they believe in God, it would probably be a very smart thing to do.

But who's doing it? Even those who you might think are doing this are constantly being uncovered, which leads us to throw up our hands and exclaim, "That's it! Nothing surprises me anymore!"

Cops are on the take, and nurses are accused of killing their patients. Catholic priests are accused of sexually molesting children. A well-known Protestant minister writes a book titled *Magnificent Marriage* and then admits committing adultery, illustrating how one can talk the talk, but not walk the walk. A TV preacher is found consorting with whores. A famous sports hero and movie star stabs his wife to death and thanks to a cockeyed jury gets away with it. Big time Washington insiders and CEOs are constantly getting nabbed for assorted swindles. Corporations and those with economic power are fleecing America through lies and various insider manipulations. Cigarette companies lie about the poison they sell to the public. People shoot members of their own family and then commit suicide. Students shoot each other in schools. Wives murder their husbands; husbands murder their wives. Adultery and pornography are now part of the accepted social scene. In the entertainment world the more gross and disgusting you become the more you are in demand. Filthy language is now commonplace in books, movies, and now even on television. People sue one another at the drop of a hat in order to make a buck even if they have no case, because there are always shyster lawyers ready to invent grievances so they can rake in a third of every settlement. And if you get into the smallest traffic accident you can assume the other guy will claim all kinds of injuries even if your speed was only 2 miles an hour.

On and on it goes, and where it ends only the Bible knows.

The Apostle Paul wrote: "Now we know that whatever the law says, it says to those who are under the law, that every mouth may be stopped, and all the world may become guilty before God" (Rom. 3:19).

"Hey, wait a minute. All the world may become guilty...Even good people are guilty?"

Wait a minute yourself. Where are you getting all these good people?

A Jewish Rabbi wrote a book titled *Why Do Bad Things Happen To Good People?*

The answer is, They don't! According to the Bible we do not live in a world of Good people and Bad people. We live in a world of Bad people. (Although it is true that some are worse than others.) The Bible says all the world is guilty...even so-called Good people whom the Bible depicts as sinners anyway. So of what value is it to be labeled Good if there is no long-range benefit to the title?

The idea of being considered guilty before God is not very appealing. People like to think of themselves as good compared to most people. And some people (the religious ones) like to think that the practice of their religion puts them one step above those who don't invest much time in the matter.

But any way you cut it, it still comes out the same. *You are guilty of sin!* You are guilty before God and at the moment you are in big trouble. A little farther on it is written, "For all have sinned and fall short of the glory of God" (Rom. 3:23).

Is it necessary to draw a picture? Sin is serious business and nothing to joke about. It can't be tossed off as unimportant. And it will not be forgiven just because you yell out to God that you are sorry ten seconds before you die. Contrary to some beliefs, it just doesn't work that way. You can even recite a prayer, or five prayers just before you die. You will still be guilty.

Sin is a tough thing to shake. Try as you might, it will be with you until the day you die. (Unless, of course, you partake of the prescribed remedy explained in your Bible and as a result nullify its final effects.)

"Every man is tempted when he is drawn away by his own desires and enticed. Then, when desire has conceived, it gives birth to sin; and sin, when it is full-grown, brings forth death" (James 1:14,15).

Sin springs from the human heart. It is not something that is picked up along the way, or something we step in, or something we catch from others. Remember the 14th verse, "...when he is drawn away by his own desires, etc." It is an inward trait.

Understanding this, one can then brush away the sophomoric teaching that "God loves the sinner, but hates the sin," as if you could somehow separate the two. Sin does not exist "over there." Sin is not something you can "leave someplace." It is ingrained within you. And it cannot exist without you. And God cannot dislike sin without disliking you.

Which brings us to another rather sensitive subject...

DOES GOD REALLY LOVE EVERYBODY...?

The God of the Bible has many characteristics and emotions, among which are: anger, compassion, wrath, hate, forgiveness, sorrow, jealousy, and of course the greatest of all, love. Love, however, is one characteristic that has for some reason become, in a way, disjointed and misunderstood.

Many knowledgeable Christians have trouble with the idea of going into an alley, coming upon a whiskey-soaked bum, and saying to him, "Hey, friend, do you know that God loves you?"

This is a popular approach to personal evangelism with certain evangelical and fundamentalist Christians, but there is a serious question as to whether it is really biblical in the strict sense of the word.

The book of Acts is a history of the early church that spans roughly thirty years, and yet in that history book you cannot find the word Love mentioned even once. This should convince us of at least two things: (1) People were not driving around the streets with God Loves You bumper stickers on the back of their chariots, and (2) personal evangelism did not consist of telling sinners that God loves them and has a wonderful plan for their lives. (Which by the way is not a spiritual law.)

The central message of the book of Acts is, "Repent therefore and be converted, that your sins may be blotted out..." (Acts 3:19). There is no example in this book of a main character going into a city and announcing that he has come to proclaim or share the love of God with anyone. They obviously did not use this approach because they did not consider it the primary message of the cross.

Surprisingly enough, the churches of today do consider this the primary message of the cross. But why?

Let's go back to our drunk in the alley. Wouldn't it make more sense to tell this fellow something like, "Hey, pal, you're in big trouble. There's a God in heaven who doesn't think too much of you and the situation you're in right now."

Wouldn't this have a better chance of grabbing his attention than hearing that God loved him—which may not necessarily be true?

If you walked up to the average person and told him that God loved him, his first reaction might be, "Well, why shouldn't He? I'm a pretty nice guy."

That response would not do him much good, but it would be the response of the self-righteous who have yet to come under conviction of their sins.

Personal conviction of sin is most important, as that is the opening which allows God's love to operate. If He is a just God, then he can truly love no other way. Divine love thrown out every which way to everyone equally is a degenerative form of love that soon becomes an easy-going, apathetic tolerance that takes very little interest in the difference between good and evil.

Furthermore, a God who is love and nothing more, a God who loves everyone always, regardless of their acts or beliefs, is not a God who could command the respect of anyone, because He would fundamentally be an unjust God who has surrendered His own standards—which is why there is no such thing as "God's unconditional love."

Time and again we read in the Bible, "Blessed is he..." and "Blessed is the man who..." and after each we usually find an admonition to become or do something. Like it or not, we have a responsibility toward action. This does not mean we work to earn God's love, but it does mean that all of us are not automatic recipients of that love.

Does the God of the Bible love the drunken bum in the alley, the Mafia godfather, and the murdering terrorist, the same way He loves the God-fearing Christian who devotes himself to prayer and honoring his creator? Does "For God so loved the world…" (John 3:16) really encompass all this? Can we rightly use a few scattered verses of this nature and with them bulldoze our way through the rest of the Bible as if no other teaching existed?

Psalm 5:5 says, "The boastful shall not stand in your sight; You hate all workers of iniquity."

Psalm 11:5 says, "The Lord tests the righteous, But the wicked and the one who loves violence His soul hates."

Evidently there are some who are not covered by the God Loves You bumper stickers. Nor in a righteous moral order, should they be.

We can engage in semantics, attempt deciphering the actual meaning of the word Hate in the original languages, and as many do, purposely sidestep the issue altogether to avoid having to face a truth with which they may not feel comfortable.

But is all this really necessary? Should not the very obvious also carry some weight? God may have a general, but definitely no *particular* love for those who by nature are children of His wrath (cf. Eph. 2:3).

Hosea says, speaking of Israel, "Because of the evil of their deeds I will drive them from My house; I will love them no more" (Hos. 9:15).

Love them no more…? Is that possible?

Evidently it is, so why play word games in order to negate the obvious? Why not let the Bible speak for itself and be content with what it teaches, and never mind defending pet doctrines that may be more acceptable for those too timid for hard thinking, or engaging in a form of "seminary-speak" that explains why the Bible doesn't really mean what it obviously says?

Psalm 78 contains some very hard language against the people of God. Israel had gone bad. They had not kept the law of God (vs. 56), they had fallen into idolatry (vs. 58), and so were given over to the sword to be killed (vs. 62). God did this because He was furious and greatly abhorred them (vs. 59).

This is definitely not how one treats people who are always loved regardless, nor is it how one chastens an object of continuous love, any more than being in Hell is the result of God's everlasting love. God discriminates between the righteous and the ungodly (Ps. 1:6, Matt. 25:46) in both this life and the life to come. Both cannot be the objects of His love. If they are then the word Love has no demonstrable meaning.

The evil sinner who reads God Loves You on the bumper sticker of the car in front of him is being sold a false bill of goods, as is the bum in the alley who hears it from a well-meaning Christian who has evidently been influenced more by radio and TV preachers than by the plain teaching of his Bible.

The early church turned the world upside down because they did not divorce the God of the Old Testament from the Christ of the New Testament. The God of the Old Testament demanded justice and held men accountable for their actions. This did not make Him a God of wrath; but it did get out the strong message that He was a God of unchanging standards.

There is nothing wrong with that. He was a strict disciplinarian who laid down the law, informed people that things had to be done His way or else, and warned that if they strayed they could get hurt. Jesus, in principle, said the same thing in many of His teachings in the four gospels.

The love of God (if understood properly) undergirds all of this. It is the mandatory foundation for God's reaching out to lost sinners.

But still, the preachers and evangelists in the book of Acts knew what they were doing when they proclaimed repentance toward God and faith in the risen Christ (Acts 20:21) as the actions that would bring newness of life—and not the initial message that God loves you. Their message demanded that the sinner make the next move.

The message God Loves You demands nothing from the sinner, and in the process turns God into a bland and harmless being who commands little respect or fear, and who needs not to be taken seriously because He loves everyone anyway.

This is not the God of the Old Testament or the Christ of the New Testament. It is instead the God of those who desire a trouble-free, easy, and flaccid Christianity that disturbs no one and costs nothing to preach. This is a weak, unscriptural God who is readily accepted by those with no understanding of who He really is.

The danger of this altered gospel of an altered God should not be underestimated.

IF YOU ARE A
HOMOSEXUAL...

...you could be in big trouble, and for one very simple reason. The Bible makes it very clear that sexual relations between persons of the same sex are outside the bounds of God's design for the human race. Homosexuality is a perversion of the norm, which means, simply put, that homosexuals are sex perverts.

"Whoa, you can't say that. That is a very bigoted and unloving thing to say. You're supposed to love other people even if you don't agree with their point of view or lifestyle."
Not necessarily. Stating a fact, that homosexuals are sex perverts, is not being unloving. It is just stating a fact, no more, no less. Al Capone was a gangster. That is a fact. It has nothing to do with being loving or unloving. Some things are facts, and some are not. What's more, if a homosexual is not a sex pervert—then who is?

The Merriam Webster's Collegiate Dictionary, tenth edition, says, under the word Pervert: "To cause to turn aside or away from what is generally done or accepted. One that has been perverted; one given to some form of sexual perversion."
Since homosexuality is not the norm, and is plainly condemned by God, then homosexuals are ungodly sex perverts. It could not be more apparent.

As far as "loving" is concerned, many Christians make the blind mistake of saying that they love homosexuals when in fact they don't even know one. Loving something or someone abstractly is loving with a love of very limited value.

Furthermore, you should not love those who are openly opposed to the standards of righteousness that God has set forth. The psalmist said, "Do I not hate them, O lord, who hate you? And do I not loathe those who rise up against you? I hate them with perfect hatred; I count them my enemies" (Ps. 139:20,21).

These are the words of a godly man, one who is so in love with God that he finds the ungodly abhorrent and wants nothing to do with them.

"Hey, doesn't the Bible say that Christians are supposed to love everybody?"

No, the Bible does not say that Christians are supposed to love everybody.

"But you're supposed to love your neighbor."

I don't have any neighbors who are homosexuals.

"Yeah, well when Jesus told the parable of the Good Samaritan, the guy the Samaritan helped didn't exactly live next door. The Samaritan found him lying in the road, and Jesus said that when the Samaritan helped the guy he was acting like a neighbor. So a homosexual doesn't have to be an actual neighbor like we usually understand the term. He just has to be in need."

Good point, but you're still wrong. If I came across a homosexual who had been mugged and was lying in the street bloody and needing help I'd stop and help the guy out of Christian compassion. But I would do absolutely nothing to help his cause or lifestyle or give the impression that I was granting him any kind of moral equivalence. To do that would be sinful on my part. An act of love toward someone does not mean that I have to love and respect that person's beliefs or lifestyle or anything else about him. I would buy a hamburger and give it to a starving Hindu, but that act would not prevent me from telling everyone that this guy's religious beliefs are off the wall and that he himself is facing spiritual disaster.

In 2nd Chron. 19:2, Jehu went before King Jehoshaphat and chewed him out, saying, "Should you help the wicked and love those who hate the Lord? Therefore the wrath of the Lord is upon you."

You are either on God's side, or on the side of the enemy. You cannot love both good and evil at the same time. Every man must choose whom he will serve.

The homosexual openly defies the law of God. God has said, "You shall not lie with a male as with a woman. It is an abomination" (Lev. 18:22). This law has just as much force as You Shall Not Steal, and You Shall Not Commit Adultery. It has never been repealed, nor has it been softened.

An "abomination" is, according to the dictionary, something odious, loathsome, and detestable. It is something that disgusts. Therefore homosexuality is not something one should feel neutral toward. It cannot—by someone who takes the Bible seriously—be considered just another lifestyle. It has to be categorized as an abomination.

"Well if homosexuality is practiced by two consenting adults who don't bother anyone else, then why should they be persecuted and denied their rights?"

No one is calling for the persecution of homosexuals any more than they are calling for the persecution of those who take the Lord's name in vain or those who do not honor their father and mother. The average Bible believing Christian is not interested in hunting down anyone. For them the existence of homosexuals is no different than the existence of bank robbers or con men. But what they do want is the right to define movements, groups, and actions according to the plain teaching of their Bibles without being called bigots, un-American, hateful members of the religious right, or that silly word "homophobic," (which can mean whatever its users decide).

Homosexuality was evidently rampant in Old Testament times, especially in those nations that God commanded Israel to clean out of the land. At times it was also found in Israel. In 1st Kings 14:22-24 the Bible records how Judah went off track and "did evil in the sight of the Lord." They built places for pagan worship on every high hill, built wooden images, and even had "perverted" people in the land, those who did "according to all the abominations of the nations that the Lord had cast out before the children of Israel."

(The notes of a good study Bible will tell you that "perverted persons" refer to male prostitutes, those who give themselves to sodomites. Both are homosexuals, and both are condemned by God.)

The New Testament changes none of this, as the condemnation is the same. In 1st Cor. 6:9,10 the Apostle Paul writes, "Do not be deceived. (In other words, don't kid yourself, pal.) Neither fornicators, nor idolaters, nor adulterers, nor homosexuals, nor sodomites…will inherit the kingdom of God."

This, then, raises a question. How can some people call themselves gay Christians if Christians will inherit the kingdom of God and homosexuals will not? How can they claim discrimination if they are barred from ordination or membership in a church, when the Bible itself (the handbook of the Christian religion) refers to them as an abomination, perverted, and totally unfit for the kingdom of God? It makes no sense.

Theoretically a Christian is someone who has left this kind of conduct behind. In 1st Cor. 6:11 it reads: "And such were some of you. But you have been washed, sanctified, justified…by the Spirit of God." In other words, that conduct is what "they"did. But when you become like "us" you no longer do this.

If the Bible is really true when it says homosexuals are unfit for the kingdom of heaven—then that's it! It makes no difference how loving a person you might be; it makes no difference how many good works you might do; it makes no difference if you're a big shot movie star or some other noteworthy artist; it makes no difference if you keep your lifestyle to yourself and don't flaunt or bother anyone else with your sexual inclinations. It doesn't even matter if you become an Episcopal Bishop.

You are doomed to Hell, because if you don't inherit the kingdom of God there is no place else to go.

Is there any hope for the homosexual?

Yes and No. There are many Christian organizations and groups that minister to homosexuals, and there are many recorded instances of Christian counseling paying big dividends. There are many who have left the homosexual lifestyle and who are now living straight lives. Some have become Bible believing Christians.

On the other hand, the Bible teaches that God has given up on many homosexuals. In Rom. 1:26 it says "God gave them up to vile passions." The word "vile" means "morally despicable, foul, degrading." Evidently this is how God views homosexual lovemaking. Considered in this light, one cannot then regard homosexuality as just another lifestyle. The next verse (27th) mentions men burning with lust for one another, committing what is shameful, and receiving in themselves the penalty of their error.

Why did all this happen? What makes men do such things? The 28th verse gives us a clue. "Because they did not like to retain God in their knowledge."

Leaving God out of one's life can, depending upon circumstances, leads to all kinds of problems. Homosexuality is evidently one of them. If there is no anchor for your soul you are capable of drifting into anything.

"...God gave them over to a debased mind, to do those things that are not fitting" (vs.28).

A debased mind...? Again the dictionary. Debased: "To cause deterioration or lowering in quality or character. Moral deterioration by evil thoughts and influences."

The homosexual, then, is one (if we may use a popular term) whose head is not screwed on right. He is a barking cat, a meowing dog, and from his debauched position he cries out for a social acceptance to which he has no right.

If the Bible is really true, and what it says about homosexuality accurate, then there is no question that current attempts by certain segments of our society to make it acceptable is in itself another perversion.

"Woe to those who call evil good and good evil; Who put darkness for light, and light for darkness" (Is. 5:20).

One tragedy of our time is how influential members of the Christian church have allowed their expanded concept of love to distort biblical fact. No one is against love. We all know the world needs more of it. But you should not use love as a force that obliterates the rest of what the Bible says, as if nothing else had claim to any importance. This approach has not delivered the results our world needs. We are not going to build the kingdom of God by wasting our time telling people they should all love one another. "Those who are in the flesh cannot please God" (Rom. 8:8) even if they love one another from now until doomsday!

If we are supposed to love the homosexual (and how one shows that is open to wide interpretation), then why don't we ever hear that we are supposed to also love bank robbers, or Mafia hit men, or terrorists who blow up planes, trains and whatnot. Do the homosexuals have better PR men, or have Christians of all denominations been conditioned by the media and society in general to be too tolerant of that which their Bible says is fundamentally intolerable?

No one advocates giving another group of citizens a hard time just because they might disagree with a particular religious belief. This is still America, the land of the free and the home of anyone who wants to follow his own drummer.

But if the Bible is really true, then those who profess to believe that Bible should be outspoken in their opposition to sin of every kind. ("Through your precepts I get understanding; Therefore I hate every false way" Ps. 119:104) They should maintain their allegiance to the laws of God and be quick to denounce those who break them. If the unlearned yell, "That's not showing love!" let them yell. Love was never meant to be a cover for wrongdoing or an excuse to ignore God's word or trample His law.

True love should seek the salvation of the homosexual. It should not be used as a cover for his sin or an excuse to not be critical. "And have no fellowship with the unfruitful works of darkness, but rather expose them" (Eph. 5:11).

THE FEAR OF THE LORD

The Bible says, "The fear of the Lord is the beginning of wisdom" (Prov. 9:10).

Fear may be a strange place to begin a lesson on wisdom. Can fearing someone actually make one a wise person?

Evidently, yes, because if a person hasn't the brains to fear God then he most likely does not have the brains to live a proper or prosperous life or ensure for himself a satisfying afterlife. He will have no incentive to avoid evil and seek holiness without which no man will see the Lord (Heb. 12:14).

There are things in life that should be feared, and intelligent people know what to fear. You should be afraid to touch live electrical wires; you should be afraid of a coming tornado; you should be afraid of a Doberman with a foaming mouth charging at you, etc. An intelligent person will fear these things and take appropriate steps to avoid them.

The Bible, however, goes a step further and claims that a healthy fear of God can keep one on a straight and narrow path. "And by the fear of the Lord one departs from evil""(Prov. 16:6). Add to this, "A wise man fears and departs from evil" (Prov. 14:16), and you have clear teaching that fearing God can be a deterrent to lawlessness.

Fearing God is the result of a mature and well-adjusted mind. And fearing God can bring health to your flesh and strength to your bones (Prov. 3:7,8), which could mean that if you want to stay healthy stay away from the wicked.

People do not usually get shot, beaten, or have their legs broken while attending church. But they can have such things happen when they consort with those for whom these things are a way of life.

Those who fear God possess a stability to their lives that can be acquired no other way. They are rooted, established, and in sync with the natural moral order. They are not spiritually dysfunctional.

Unfortunately the fear of God is not taught in many of our churches. They would rather talk about God's love for everyone, the good, the bad, and the ugly. It's so very comforting to talk about love, so very peaceful. It makes us all one big happy family.

But we are not all one big happy family. The Bible teaches that if we do not fear the Lord we are one big foolish family—because the fear of the Lord is the beginning of wisdom!

Most nonfiction magazine writers learn one thing very early in their careers, which is: If you want to make money selling to magazines the fastest and easiest way is to write about one of the Big Three, money, sex, or health.

This is because most people feel they should have (or could use) more money; most people think their love life could be better or more exciting than it is; and no one wants to get sick and end up in the hospital, and maybe die. Obviously, then, any article on one of these subjects will be of interest to the average reader.

We live in a "me" oriented generation. It was once said, "Whatever is good for General Motors is good for the USA." It is now generally understood (even among some Christians) that "Whatever is good for me comes first and the world and everyone else can go hang."

This is obviously not the biblical view. Satisfaction cannot be found in a "me" oriented life. If you doubt that, consider the writer in the book of Ecclesiastes. He searched for pleasure, joy, and satisfaction everywhere, but found nothing of lasting value. He finally decided that the conclusion of the whole matter was to "Fear God and keep His commandments, for this is mans' all" (meaning, his basic duty) Ecc.12:13.

Fearing God and keeping His commandments is a God oriented way of life, and a life that brings God's blessing. People are not blessed because they have figured out (via a string of Bible verses) how to handle various problems we all experience. There is no real evidence for this kind of thinking, and it is not central in the teachings of Christ.

Yet within the church people seem obsessed with the Big Three. The average Christian is not dead to the world. On the contrary, he is very much alive and tuned into it. His love life, finances, and health are all that really matter, and fortunately (?) for him there is a steady stream of books and magazine articles available geared to enhancing his life in these and other areas.

But books like: *Will The Real Me Please Stand Up?...52 Ways To Get Your Life And House In Order...The Search For Significance...Building Your Mates Self Esteem...*and *Taming Tension,* etc., are all ego centered and of little value to the spiritual life of the average Christian. Then we have the steady stream of books by "plastic" Christian celebrity authors that teach us little more than How to Have a Nice and Successful Day.

To all this the writer in Ecclesiastes says "Nuts!" It's all vanity and grasping for the wind (Ecc. 1:14,17). Jesus did not die for this.

This does not mean we cannot benefit in a peripheral manner from the basic gospel message. We can. But why not first follow the clear teaching of the Bible when seeking to be blessed in this life?

Example: "Blessed is the man who fears the Lord, Who delights greatly in His commandments" (Ps. 112:1). (This verse could be considered an embodiment of the true Christian life. It's worth memorizing and meditating upon. If you lived like this you would be right on target.) To be blessed is to have good things happen to you. When the patriarchs and leaders of Israel blessed the people they called down God's favor and benefits upon them.

In this verse it is our attitude and reaction to God that determines our blessing, and not how we manipulate certain Bible verses in an attempt to find the right key that will bring us good times and emotional stability. The latter has a tendency to make God a usable and then disposable commodity, while the former gives God a rightful place as Lord of our lives and dispenser of the blessings that are gifts of His grace.

There is a huge difference between the two.

The fear of the Lord is the beginning of wisdom—and knowledge (Prov. 1:7). If you do not begin here then you cannot obtain the wisdom and knowledge needed to effectively run your life. This is why so many people float around like ships without a rudder. They try guiding their lives with various theories and programs that will supposedly unlock the secrets of happy living, whereas they should first humble themselves in fear before the majesty of the Lord.

Again in Ecclesiastes the writer says, "Though a sinner does evil a hundred times, and his days are prolonged, yet I surely know that it will be well with those who fear God, who fear before Him" (Ecc. 8:12).

Doesn't this make it clear that living in the fear of God is the most sensible thing a person can do? Abraham was blessed because he feared God (Gen. 22:12), and not because he had gained insight into his love life, or his finances, or his health. He did not manufacture his own blessings by using spiritual formulas.

They were given to him because he walked in the fear of the Lord!

Moses said to the children of Israel, "And now, Israel, what does the Lord your God require of you, but to fear the Lord your God, to walk in all His ways..." (Deut. 10:12). The psalmist said, "The Lord takes pleasure in those who fear Him" (Ps. 147:11).

And lest one think this is just Old Testament mentality, in 1 Pet. 1:17 it says that Christians, while they are on this earth, should be conducting themselves in fear. The admonition to walk in the fear of the Lord is also given in Acts 9:31. The one who walks in the fear of the Lord walks with his head screwed on right. This is a simple, biblical, and basic teaching of the Bible. It is also the way of blessing.

Christians should forget the amateur pulpit psychiatrists and writers who claim that by sprinkling Bible verses over your natural instincts you can manipulate them for your benefit. That is the religion of those who find their theology in the pages of The National Enquirer and Reader's Digest, etc., and not in their Bibles.

Should not a person fear the judgment of God? Is the judgment of God upon sin so trivial we can afford to give it only passing interest? The Bible seems very clear on the matter. If you ignore God's salvation you can expect God's judgment, and that judgment is something to be feared. The following Bible verses are well worth mentioning:

"For if we sin willfully after we have received the knowledge of the truth, there no longer remains a sacrifice for sins, but a certain fearful expectation of judgment, and fiery indignation which will devour the adversaries. Anyone who rejected Moses' law dies without mercy on the testimony of two or three witnesses. Of how much worse punishment do you suppose, will he be thought worthy of who has trampled the Son of God underfoot, counted the blood of the covenant by which he was sanctified a common thing, and insulted the Spirit of grace? For we know Him who said, 'Vengeance is mine, I will repay,' says the Lord. And again, 'The Lord will judge His people.' It is a fearful thing to fall into the hands of the living God" (Heb. 10:26-31).

So you see, you could be in big trouble! The fiery indignation of God might very well devour you if you are not one of His children, but rather an adversary.

There is a companion verse to the one just quoted, and it is spoken by Jesus. "But I will show you whom you should fear; Fear Him who, after He has killed, has power to cast into Hell; yes, I say to you, fear Him" (Luke 12:5).

After He has killed…? God is responsible for the death of certain people? He kills people…?

Evidently, yes. But we don't usually hear about God in that context. That's a bit hard, isn't it? Well, maybe, but the Bible does say that God has the power to kill and then cast into Hell. Worry about that and never mind what some pious clergyman spews out in the paper or at some public event, or from his pulpit, about God worrying over you because you came down with the flu, or because your car battery died. Most of them of are in the business of comforting you.

The Bible is in the business of warning you!

Consider the following: In 1st Samuel 2:22-25 we are told that Eli the priest was getting old and that his sons were sinning wickedly with the women who came to the tabernacle. Eli argues that they should stop messing around because they are causing the Lord's people to sin. But the sons paid no attention to their father's words *because the Lord desired to kill them.*

Now how do you figure that? Well, evidently these fellows had gone past the point of no return. God had decided that enough was enough. He would kill them and get them out of the way. This is not a pleasant thought, but instances like this happen.

(Hey, reader, is there any chance that God might have plans on the drawing board to kill you because of the way you've been living? The next time you hear of some young kids getting killed by wrapping their car around a telephone pole at 90mph there might be more to the story than just a heavy foot on the accelerator.)

You will probably never find Luke 12:5 on any kind of note paper or inspirational card, but if you did and sent it to someone you would be doing the person to whom it was sent the biggest favor of his/her life. No one fears God any more, and that is exactly why our society and societies around the world are rotting from corruption and immorality.

"The fear of the Lord is a fountain of life to turn one away from the snares of death" (Prov. 14:27). Does that sound as if Fear is supposed to be some kind of deterrent? It should, because that's exactly the way the verse should be understood.

"Hold on, sport. Doesn't the Bible say you are supposed to obey God out of love?"

Not exactly. That sounds good in a catechism or Sunday school class, but when one considers the overall teaching of the Bible it's tough to support. Consider Phil. 2:12 where it says to Christians, "Therefore, my beloved, as you have always obeyed, not as in my presence only, but now much more in my absence, work out your own salvation *with fear and trembling*." Furthermore, there isn't a non-Christian on earth who is capable of obeying God out of love. Their minds do not work that way (Rom. 8:7).

When one fears God he does not mess around, he does not cook up evil schemes, he does not seek to take advantage of others, he does not rob convenience stores, kill people, talk his neighbor's wife into meeting him at a motel, whatever… He walks the straight and narrow road of righteousness, and hates that which dishonors his Lord.

You cannot fear God and fellowship with evil with any degree of comfort. We cannot, or course, escape the presence of evil while we live in this world. We must do business with evil (people) every day just in order to survive. But our attitude toward evil should be one of pure loathing. The righteous man should not merge with that which is sinful and wrong in order to feel or be accepted by the world. Instead, he should be quick to point out the sin or immorality of any situation regardless of who might be offended. This is something rarely done by the average Christian because he is afraid of being labeled judgmental. Our present society has made him cower in social impotence.

But the one who has confidence in his God and knows the Word of God will not shrink from this holy calling. We have been called to be Jeremiahs and John the Baptists; we have been called to be the salt of the earth; we have been called to point a finger and to speak out. Didn't Jesus do this?

But first make sure you know exactly what you are talking about, and how you are living your own life, as there is no bigger fool, and no one more destructive to the cause of Christ, than a self-righteous hypocrite.

THE ANGEL OF DEATH

Is there really an angel of death, a heavenly "hit man" who kills people at God's command?

The Bible indicates there may be. God destroys people and armies and does it with the assistance of angels who have been given that job. One of the most notable instances can be found in the story of the first Passover in Ex. 12:12-23. God told the children of Israel that each household should kill a lamb, eat it, and take some of its blood and put it on the doorposts of the house in which the lamb is eaten. Then He said:

"For I will pass through the land of Egypt on that night, and will strike all the firstborn in the land of Egypt, both man and beast; and against all the gods of Egypt I will execute judgment: I am the Lord.

"Now the blood shall be a sign for you on the houses where you are. And when I see the blood, I will pass over you; and the plague shall not be on you to destroy you when I strike the land of Egypt" (vs. 12,13).

God reveals that He is going to kill the firstborn of everything in Egypt as punishment because Pharaoh would not let His people go.

But when we look deeper into the incident (vs. 23) we find out exactly how this is accomplished. This verse reads, "For the Lord will pass through to strike the Egyptians; and when He sees the blood on the lintel and on the two doorposts, the Lord will pass over the door and not allow the destroyer to come into your house to strike you."

Evidently it is someone else who does the actual killing, although it is at the express command of God. The destroyer is obviously an angelic being who does the Lord's bidding.

Another vivid example of the destroyer at work can be found in 2nd Sam. 24:15,16 where it is recorded, "So the Lord sent a plague upon Israel from the morning till the appointed time. From Dan to Beersheba seventy thousand men of the people died. And when the angel stretched out his hand over Jerusalem to destroy it the Lord relented from the destruction, and said to the angel who was destroying the people, 'It is enough; now restrain your hand.'"

No, angels are not just cherub-faced creatures who hover over scenes on Christmas cards, or who escort the souls of the dearly departed into Paradise. No. Depending upon the circumstances, they can be deadly killers whose power is unimaginable.

The very idea of angels being destroyers can be frightening. It goes against so much of our preconceived thinking. And whether it is only one angel who has this power, or many, we cannot be sure. When the Bible says, "…nor complain, as some of them also complained, and were destroyed by the destroyer" (1st Cor. 10:10), it sounds as if we are talking about one specific individual…but we really don't know.

In Ps 78:49, when contemplating upon God's dealings with Egypt at the time of the exodus, the writer states: "He cast on them the fierceness of His anger, wrath, indignation, and trouble, By sending angels of destruction among them."

So maybe we have more than one; or maybe all angels are involved, depending upon the situation….

When they do get involved their power seems almost limitless. In Is. 37 the king of Assyria is threatening Israel and king Hezekiah, saying the gods of other nations had not saved them from his armies, so what makes Hezekiah think that his God will be any more effective?

Hezekiah takes the letter from the opposing king and spreads it before the Lord asking Him to save Jerusalem from the Assyrians. God answers, "For I will defend this city, to save it for my own sake and for my servant David's sake" (vs. 35).

How then does God defend the city of Jerusalem? Verse 36 describes the mechanics of the operation:

"Then the angel of the Lord went out and killed (in one night) in the camp of the Assyrians one hundred and eighty-five thousand; and when the people arose early in the morning, there were the corpses—all dead."

This is amazing. Exactly how this angel killed is not explained. But the word "killed" here means literally Struck, and that usually indicates death by the sword. But again, exactly how this took place is not explained. It is enough to know that according to the Bible one angel killed in one night 185,000 men. And all this at the command of God.

Angels did not kill only in Old Testament times. During the early days of the church Herod the king decided to harass certain elements of the church. He killed James, the brother of John, and because it pleased the Jews he threw Peter into prison.

Herod thought he was real big stuff. In Acts 12:21 he decked himself out and sat on his throne to give a big speech. The people cried out in adoration, "The voice of a god and not of man!"

But Herod was no god. An angel of the Lord struck him (vs. 22) and he was eaten by worms and died. So much for pretenders to the throne.

In the book of Psalms it is written, "Bless the Lord, you His angels, Who excel in strength, who do His word, Heeding the voice of His word. Bless the Lord, all you His hosts, you ministers of His who do His pleasure" (Ps. 103:20,21).

Angels exist to serve God. When God wants something done they execute His will—whatever it is.

At the second coming of Christ it is the angels whom Jesus will send to gather His elect from the four corners of the earth (cf. Matt. 24:31), and it is the angels who will "pour out the bowls of the wrath of God on the earth" (Rev. 16:1-17). It is an angel carrying a great chain in his hand who will bind Satan and cast him into the bottomless pit for a thousand years.

Consider this: Those angels who come at the end of this age to gather together those who belong to Jesus "And He will send His angels with a great sound of a trumpet, and they will gather together His elect from the four winds, from one end of Heaven to the other" (Matt. 24:31), well, they might be carrying big clipboards with lists of names. If your name is not on their list then I can guarantee that you are in big trouble.

JUDGE OR BE PREPARED TO BE JUDGED

An often misquoted verse of Scripture is "Judge not that you be not judged" (Matt. 7:1). Many people consider only the surface meaning of this verse. They feel it is improper to ever speak negatively about anybody or anything. "Who are you to judge?" they say.

But it all depends upon the kind of judgment you are making. Matt. 7:1 teaches that we are not to pass judgment upon Joe Doe's character or motives, because when you judge these apparent flaws, you could be blind to your own that might be worse. If you get picky with Joe he could get picky with you, and you might then find yourself on the short end of the stick.

Furthermore, you are not acting merciful when you judge others. Luke 6:36 says, "Therefore be merciful, just as your Father in heaven is merciful." And verse 37 continues: "Judge not, and you shall not be judged. Condemn not, and you shall not be condemned."

And yet in 1st Cor. 5 we find a whole chapter on how church members should judge one another. (Now how do you like that?) In light of Matt. 7:1 that might sound very contradictory, but it isn't. Matt. 7:1-5 does not deal with how a church should conduct itself. It deals instead in a generalized way with criticizing the actions of your neighbor. It was spoken to people devoid of the Spirit of God and moral enlightenment. The Bible *does* grant

Christians the right to judge sin where sin has clearly been defined and committed.

In 1st Cor. 5 the Corinthians were to pass judgment upon an individual's sin—and then throw him out of the church. Could you imagine an incident of this nature getting on your local TV news? Immediately TV reporters (who usually know nothing about religion or spiritual matters) would side with the one being disciplined. We would hear: (1) He is being thrown out of a church where all should be welcome. (2) What member of this church will come out and throw the first stone? (3) Is this an example of love? (4) These stiff-necked and self-righteous fundamentalists have set themselves up as judge and jury. (5) If Jesus were here would He throw people out of the church because they weren't perfect?

And on it would go, with no thought as to whether or not a church has the right to maintain its moral, ethical, or doctrinal standards in order to keep itself from spiritual pollution, or whether it should heed the warning that a little leaven can leaven the whole lump (cf. 1st Cor. 5:5,6). The TV reporters would not worry about the church's standards or even be aware that they exist. Their focus would be on the disciplined individual who is standing like a lonely David against the church Goliath. He makes better copy. Forget that he might have molested the choir leader's young daughter, or arrived at an evening service stone drunk, or got caught stealing from the collection plates. That is not the issue.

For the media the main issue would be: "Who do these narrow-minded bigots think they are throwing someone out of the church? These born-again whackos are becoming a cultural menace. Isn't a church supposed to be a meeting place for sinners?"

Well…not really. Actually, a church is a showcase for saints. But you would rarely, if ever, find anyone in the media who would understand that.

Putting someone out of the church is a hard call to make, and you must know all the facts before undertaking such a move. But the Apostle Paul called upon the believers in 1st Cor. 5 to do exactly that. Those who would someday judge angels were to sit in judgment upon each other.

Passing judgment upon the beliefs of others is another area in which many Christians are hesitant to act. Matt. 7:15,16 reads, "Beware of false prophets who come to you in sheep's clothing, but inwardly they are ravenous wolves. You will know them by their fruits...."

If we are to know someone by his fruits, then we have to make a judgment as to whether the fruit is good or bad. This is a moral responsibility that has been entrusted to us. You should not shirk this responsibility by flinching before those who cry, "But who are you to judge? We have not been called to be fruit inspectors."

Let me tell you who you are to judge. You are someone with a working knowledge of the Bible. You understand the great doctrines of the faith. As one who takes the Bible seriously you have a certain degree of spiritual wisdom (1st Cor. 2:10-15). If you cannot judge truth from error, who can?

Rom. 16:17 reads, "Now I urge you, brethren, note those who cause divisions and offenses contrary to the doctrine which you have learned, and avoid them." But how can you do that unless you first pass judgment on their beliefs?

Those who take the Bible seriously have to discern and judge. In fact much of their Christian experience should consist of weeding out the good from the bad. And if that isn't judging, then what is? Our pagan society does not want anyone judging it. Make a judgment and someone will be quick to cry, "Doesn't your Bible say you shouldn't go around judging others?"

Your answer should be, "Not necessarily. The whole Bible is a judgment upon our world. Read it for yourself and you will find the writers making all kinds of judgments upon the actions and beliefs of others."

In 2nd John, verse 10, the Bible says, "If anyone comes to you and does not bring this (the correct) doctrine, do not receive him into your house, nor greet him."

How's that for judging others? It sounds hard, but these are judgments the writers of the New Testament told their followers to make. Do you shy away from this because you do not want to be found judging or criticizing others?

You shouldn't, because these Bible verses are just as much a part of the Bible as the verse that says we should love our neighbors.

Those who make no judgment at all show themselves morally worthless insofar as affecting the good of their society. And the most worthless Christian of all is one who will hide behind the cry, "Who am I to judge or criticize?" This person is afraid (or unable) to publicly distinguish truth from error. He will eventually come to feel uncomfortable in the presence of others who are more discerning and willing to judge. He will allow truth and error, right and wrong, and good and evil to get mixed in the same bag. This bag we could label Moral Agnosticism. The world might find it comfortable living with this bag. Those who take the Bible seriously should find it abhorrent!

The Apostle Paul prayed that the love of the Philippians would abound still more and more in knowledge and all discernment (Phil. 1:9). Love cannot be effective when it operates in ignorance. Know the Bible, study its doctrines and teachings, and then make your stand and judge with righteous judgment, for he who is spiritual has the right to judge all things (cf. 1st Cor. 2:15).

For those who are not students of the Word of God, when someone with some biblical knowledge says to you, "Hey, what you are doing (or believe) is dead wrong," don't start yelling that he shouldn't be judging others. He might be right in what he is saying.

And if he is—you could be in big trouble.

WHAT IS A CHURCH?

If the Bible is really true then there can only be one true church, because there is only one true belief. There may be minor variations in how different parts of this one true church functions, but there cannot be differing beliefs.

A Bible dictionary will define the word Church as: "A local assembly of believers as well as the redeemed of all ages who follow Jesus Christ as Savior and Lord."

The true church is therefore composed of people who are heading for heaven when they die. They are saints. Followers of God are referred to by this name throughout the Bible, although its meaning is developed more fully in the New Testament. A saint, by definition, is one who has been set apart and become pure. Believers are called saints in Rom. 1:7 and Phil. 1:1, the latter reading, "To all the saints in Christ Jesus who are at Philippi…"

Needless to say, the church of Jesus Christ is composed of a very special group of people. They believe certain things, they follow Jesus Christ, they have been redeemed, and as saints they have been, at the present time, set apart and sanctified. As members of this one true church they have three major functions. (1) To evangelize the world, (2) to edify one another, (3) to guard the truth.

Those who are not members of this church have a problem (of which they are usually unaware).

Unfortunately in our present time the popular religious trend is the ecumenical movement that is trying to promote worldwide Christian unity, and in some cases just plain religious unity. Beliefs matter little to the pure ecumenist because they can be divisive. He would rather concentrate on love, a love that supersedes any form of doctrinal belief.

The main problem here is that an organization based on nothing more than love for one another can never be a church. It is, at best, nothing more than a "nice guy's club."

"Yeah, but in there people care for and love one another. Isn't that the very essence of Christianity?"

No, it is not! You can care for and love one another all the way to Hell. Being a nice member of a nice group that does many nice things will guarantee you nothing. Groups of nice people do not make a church. And a church is not just a group of nice people who might also be religious.

"But isn't it at least a step in the right direction…?"

No. It's more a step in the wrong direction. People who are "nice" according to the world's standards, and who see religious value in that "niceness," will be less inclined to repent of their sins and seek a savior.

A church—according to the Bible—is a congregation of the redeemed. And the redeemed are those who have been saved from the penalty of their sins through faith in the shed blood of Christ as payment for their iniquities. If you are not a member of that group you can walk into a church every Sunday until the day you die and it will do you no good. You have not been saved and therefore you are lost.

If that sounds hard, remember that the Bible is a very hard book. It makes no allowances for nice guys or good intentions, nor does it bend to accommodate current standards or beliefs.

But there will always be those who are going to do things their way regardless of who might not like it. They are oftentimes (but not always) found in small towns under the name The Community (or Federated) Church, or something similar. Their main belief is that there is no point in being dogmatic about your beliefs. The emphasis here is to get along with everyone and minister to others in whatever way you can by helping them with their problems and needs.

That might be a good program for the local chapter of Elks, or the Rotary Club, or the local United Way, or whatever benevolent group you have in town, but it is not the function of a true Christian church. If you can help solve someone's problem that's a good thing to do; if you can help someone straighten out his life that's a good thing to do; if you loan your time and energy to a good cause that's a good thing to do. If as a Christian you can do these things then by all means do them.

But if you think that by doing these things, or five times the amount of these things, under the banner of some amorphous Christian movement, that this makes you a Christian, you are sadly mistaken.

There is no atoning value in social activism or benevolent organizations no matter how noble the cause. If there were then Christ died for nothing.

Cities and towns across America have been infected with the idea that religion for the sake of religion, and church cooperation for the sake of cooperation, is the way to go. Ministers from various denominations have rushed to join small groups whose purpose is to break down denominational barriers.

"Yes, but now they can understand each other better, and become more appreciative, more respectful, and more knowledgeable about each other's faith."

So what? What does all this do for the average guy in the pew? Who is going to Heaven and avoiding Hell because of this?

"Yeah, but—"

Hold it just a minute. This is nothing more than playing church. It's a hobby for clergymen who unfortunately can't think of anything better to do with their time. They would be better off devising programs to reach lost sinners than fooling around with this stuff that affects no one but themselves.

These misguided individuals are constantly dreaming up ways to hold joint Thanksgiving services, or making joint pronouncements at the local food pantry, or getting involved in religiously coated community projects. It's "surface do-goodism" at its best.

But it's Christianity at its worst! The early church did not turn the world upside down with this stuff. If you should come across a church with a sign out front that says something like, "We care about people and their needs and want you to experience the love of God in your life by joining with others like yourself," you might be better off to keep driving.

But if the sign said something like, "We preach Christ crucified, risen, and coming again," the chances would be better that this is a church that knows and preaches the basics of the faith. This would be a church worth investigating.

Ecumenism does nothing for the average churchgoing individual. It is a game played by professionals that has to do with power, control, and ego. Churches that understand and respect the Word of God from front to back have little if anything to do with the movement for the simple reason that the movement itself ministers to no one and only breeds doctrinal confusion. (Assuming anyone in the movement cares about biblical doctrine in the first place.) Plus, it does not have a central message that engenders conversion to the gospel message.

So who needs it?

However, churches that do believe the complete Bible is really true, are not without their faults. One of the main faults is with those who have risen in the ranks and have taken on the mantle of Christian celebrity. This individual will have written a few books and had his picture in some of the top evangelical magazines. He usually gives out with a steady stream of advice that is supposed to make the rest of us happier, more well-adjusted, free from emotional problems, and very thankful that we are Christians. He might even have his own TV show on one of the Christian cable channels.

But his approach to everyday problems is really more psychiatric than spiritual. In fact much of what he says can be found in secular periodicals that fill supermarket newsstands. But his material is somewhat different in that it contains Bible quotes. This supposedly makes his material Christian.

But it doesn't make it Christian—it makes it religious, because the use (and misuse) of Scripture does not make something Christian if it has no direct connection to the gospel message. Do you want to teach people to be nice and to help feed the poor? Fine, go ahead, and throw in a few Bible verses to that effect. But this is more religious than it is Christian because it does not deal with the issues of spiritual life or spiritual death.

If people are Christians first (possessing spiritual life) and then you teach them how to be nice and feed the poor, then you have something going for you. You have things in the right order that can produce the right fruit.

There is only one true gospel, but there are many presentations of religious belief and experience. It is the individual's responsibility to weed out the good from the bad, the true from the false. If the Bible is really true, then you have a responsibility to search it diligently to find the true gospel and the way to everlasting life.

The foundation of the Christian life is the message of Christ and Him crucified. This message is not supposed to rejuvenate, reform, or through some aspect of Christian teaching bring us into a right relationship with ourselves and others. No, we are to die to ourselves so we can be brought into a right relationship with God.

Yes, it follows that this right relationship with God should overflow and affect our dealings with others. But too often we find this Celebrity pushing the view that Christianity has something to do with enabling us to better adjust to our present life, our spouse, our job, our in-laws, and the world in general. The untrained mind could get the false impression that this "right way of living and looking at things" is the very basis of the Christian experience.

But it is not.

This new Celebrity is a builder, but not one who lays foundations. He rarely takes on opponents of the faith because he does not wish to anger anyone. This would not enhance his celebrity. Because of this the secular world takes little notice of him because he is harmless. He is no threat. Only church people listen to him. In one sense the rulers of our culture appreciate his ministry because he takes the mind of the people and focuses it upon themselves instead of on truths that would threaten their control.

The Celebrity's followers are usually quite parochial in their outlook. Few of them know how to think or define spiritual truth for themselves. They don't find this necessary as the Celebrity does all their thinking for them.

The Celebrity is in the business of building mature Christians, therefore he feels it necessary to straighten out their marriages, their relationship with the boss at work, the next door neighbor, and most important of all, their understanding of themselves. To do this he plays the role of family psychiatrist, which is usually done under the guise of Christian counseling. For him this is deep stuff, so much more challenging than a simple presentation of the gospel. He is above that. The basics of the faith he leaves to the beginners, those preachers who have not advanced to his level.

The foundation of the Christian faith is of course Jesus Christ. This foundation has been laid by those who teach salvation through the blood of the cross, that through Christ's shed blood sinners are saved from Hell and made righteous, and that they now inherit eternal life.

If the Christian has this solid foundation in his heart, his next step is to grow in the faith and to be stable, so as not to be tossed about and influenced by every strange belief beckoning at every turn in the road.

It is here where the Celebrity misses the boat. Instead of training the newly converted in the great doctrines of the faith, instead of equipping him with the tools of spiritual warfare, instead of building his inner life of prayer and meditation on the Word, the Celebrity instead gets the Christian to focus on himself and his emotional and family problems. Every quirk, idiosyncrasy, fit of depression and minor emotional issue that pops up now becomes the object of intense scrutiny.

On this the Celebrity builds. The Christian is now concerned with himself and his own personal problems, and now embarks upon his own selfish little ego trip, convinced that Jesus died to give him the ability to make of himself, through the proper application of certain Bible passages, a better, more well-adjusted individual.

But this is all straw that will not endure under the testing of God's refining fire. It is spiritual trivia of the worst sort. The Christian message is not the good news of self-realization, or emotional stability, or happy marriages.

It deals with issues of much more importance. Eternal importance. If any form of so-called Christian teaching does not connect in some way with the basics then it is just so much stubble meant to be burned. The Celebrity who spends all this time promoting this "side issue trivia" will in the end find his works burned and his reward lost (cf. 1st Cor. 3:11-15).

There is an Old Testament verse that says, "To the law and to the testimony! If they do not speak according to this word, it is because there is no light in them" (Is. 8:20). This is an answer to the previous verse that warned against seeking out advice from wizards and mediums who would contact the dead for information. The writer is saying, basically, "Don't waste your time listening to those who are not speaking to you from the Word of God. They walk in darkness and do not have the light of truth."

Anyone who gives any kind of spiritual advice or teaching that is not biblically based should be ignored. You cannot overemphasize the importance of establishing every doctrine and belief on the written Word of God. Extra biblical sources of teaching, even if promoted by respected (in the eyes of the world) clergymen, should be held suspect. You don't need theories formulated in a seminary or seminar; you need the teaching that follows, "Thus says the Lord..."

This is the law and the testimony. This is "...the word to your servant upon which you have cause me to hope. This is my comfort in my affliction, For your word has given me life" (Ps 119:49,50).

And this is the word upon which the true church of Jesus Christ is built. You owe it to yourself to be part of it.

DO WE ALL WORSHIP THE SAME GOD?

We have heard it many times, usually from someone not well versed in the Bible, but who means well. There is a religious discussion of sorts, differences are pointed out concerning various beliefs, and then someone will say, "Well, we all worship the same God anyway."

Unfortunately that is not true. We do not all worship the same God. You either worship the God who has revealed Himself in the Bible, or you do not worship any god—because there is no other God. If you do worship an entity that is alive and who responds to you, you can be sure it is demonic in nature

This simple truth is not very well understood in this day of religious pluralism and equality. People are told that there are many roads to God, and that these roads are different ways of worship.

There's only one thing wrong with this picture. The God of the Bible never said this! But since many people (including some who attend church regularly) never read the Bible anyway, it's not too surprising that they are unaware of this simple fact.

In the Old Testament there was no belief that "We all worship the same God anyway." In 2nd Kings 5:15 the Syrian commander, Naaman, after being healed of his leprosy, said to Elisha the prophet, "Indeed, now I know that there is no God in all the earth, except in Israel..." meaning, of course, that not only were all other deities worthless, but also that none of them were representative of the true God.

At that time there were many pagan gods in the earth known by a number of names. No Israelite would ever dream of saying that those who worshipped Molech or Dagon are really worshipping the Lord God of Israel, but in their own way. Even Naaman knew this, and he said later in vs.18 that he did not want it held against him when he went into the temple of Rimmon with his master the king. And when he bowed to Rimmon (as he had to under the circumstances) he asked also to be pardoned for this.

Naaman now knew that Rimmon was no god, but instead a fake, an invention of someone's mind. And he implicitly knew that the true God would not be pleased with this kind of worship.

How different it is today when so many professing Christians look with tolerance and respect upon other forms of worship and doctrinal beliefs that are diametrically opposed to Scripture.

"Yeah, but some people have different ways of worshipping God. It's narrow to think there is only one way to God."

Yes, it may seem narrow. But if the Bible is really true—it is also very correct.

If the Bible is really true it demands more allegiance than the stray opinions of men. "Nor is there salvation in any other, for there is no other name under heaven given among men by which we must be saved" (Acts 4:12), was spoken by the Apostle Peter about Jesus. It is either true…or it isn't. It cannot be both true and false. What it means is that there is no value in following Molech or Dagon or Allah or Buddha or Baal or Zeus or any other religious leader who claims to be speaking the truth. You can only find your salvation in Jesus Christ. If the Bible is really true you must adjust to this. In fact you have to, or you will perish.

When a Christian looks with favor upon any other form of belief or worship it opens the door to compromise and eventual apostasy. False worship is false—period! It is not a way of looking at the truth from a different perspective, nor is it a system that has been set up with God's approval to reach those who have not yet been exposed to the true gospel.

In 1st Cor.10:14-22, the Apostle Paul warns Christians against having anything to do with false worship, as false worship is demonic and of the devil. Satan has many ways to turn a person's mind from the truth, and the most subtle way is to clothe his perversions with religious trappings. If we grant any legitimacy (or respect) to false worship we lose the opportunity to distinguish publicly between truth and error, and this is always to the detriment of those who might be seeking the truth.

A Christian cannot claim to worship the one true God, and then say that members of other beliefs are approaching the same God in their own way, and that God understands and will accept them even if they are somewhat off base in their theology.

There isn't one line in any Bible translation in existence that supports that kind of thinking!

That, rather, is the belief of the ecumenist and his hordes of biblically illiterate followers who have set aside God's standards and have instead manufactured their own. The ecumenist says we all worship the same God because his god is a fine old fellow who believes in fair play, love, social justice, the rights of the oppressed, and the latest public opinion polls.

But this is not the God of the Bible. This is the God of the TV network newsmen who like to think they are making the world a better place by publicizing the right kind of God who wants to promote peace and understanding, and who wants to sweep out of the way everything that opposes the brotherhood of man and peace on earth, and whose main goal should be ending all kinds of discrimination and everything else that seems unfair and wrong according to present day thinking.

The God of the Bible, however, says that He is opposed to the philosophy of this world. He warns about a Day of Judgment, He warns about personal sins, and He says there is a "god of this age" (2nd Cor.4:4), and a "prince of the power of the air" (Eph. 2:2), running things down here at the moment with whom He is not associated. He (Jesus) said that if His followers thought like everyone else in the world, the world would love them; but because He chose them out of the world (making them opposed to worldly thinking and standards) the world will hate them (cf. John 15:19).

Obviously there are two different standards here and one of them has to be wrong.

The mind of God—like it or not—is disclosed in the Bible, and not in the latest religious polls or pronouncements of ecclesiastical leaders.

To assert, for even a moment, that other beliefs have any legitimacy is to deny the personal holiness of God, the Bible (His word), and the specific claims of Jesus Christ. A lack of proper teaching on biblical separation and other doctrinal matters has led many to suppose that God has both lowered and loosened His standards and doesn't take His own word seriously.

But God does take His word seriously. Jesus did not constantly quote the Old Testament for nothing. He did not always say, "It is written" if what was written did not mean something important. When you buy into Christianity you buy into the whole package, and not just that which pleases you for the moment. Those who follow the latter path are, according to the Bible, deceived and lost, victims of their own ignorance and/or stubbornness, which is why there are going to be many upset and disappointed people on judgment day.

"But if they follow their own religion perfectly won't that at least count for something?"

No, it won't count for something. It will count for nothing!

"Where's your compassion? It seems to me---"

Here we go with the "It seems to me" business. Haven't you been paying attention? My compassion is giving out the gospel message, supporting missionaries, whatever it takes to win the lost. I care about people, especially my loved ones. Will I be helping them by telling them there might be something good in some jerk religion?

Not only will following the wrong religion get you nowhere, but following the right religion wrong can also be a disaster. In Gal.1:8 it is written, "But even if we or an angel from heaven, preach any other gospel to you than what we have preached to you, let him be accursed."

Now, who is the "we" the writer is talking about? The "we" is obviously the clergy, the ones running Christianity at the time. The writer (the Apostle Paul) is saying: "If you hear anything new from any of us don't pay any attention, because it's wrong. What we have already given you is the right gospel, and cursed is the guy who changes it around."

Then he mentions the possibility of an angel from heaven preaching something else. Now I'll have to admit that if I ran into a real angel and he was giving out some information that he told me was very important, I'd be hard pressed to ignore him. Yet the Apostle Paul is telling me that's exactly what I would have to do. The angel is a fake and his message is wrong and he is accursed.

"Are you nuts? You'd ignore an angel just because he doesn't preach everything exactly the way you first heard it?"

I would have to. And I don't care what stunts he pulled off to back up his teaching. If his 100-foot shimmering image showed up on the side of a glass skyscraper and a voice came out saying, "If you want to gain salvation you must eat spinach twice a week," I'm sure the crowds would be miles deep. People would be flying in from all over the world to see this phenomenon. The stores would be sold out of spinach. The TV networks would cancel all regular programming to cover this. Deluded liberal clergymen would be calling this a new day in religious thinking.

And I would be saying to myself, "But the Bible warns against this very thing. These poor fools don't know what they're doing."

And I would be right.

There is only one gospel, one correct message, one set of true doctrines. If I were to deviate from them I would do so at my peril. Yes, I know. That's rather tight thinking. But if the Bible is really true as it is written, I dare not do otherwise.

IS THERE SPIRITUAL BLINDNESS?

Many Christians are frustrated by the inability of others to understand and perceive the simple truths of the Christian faith. They offer what they feel is the most important information a person can hear, in a simple and straightforward manner. Surely everyone to whom the gospel is intelligently explained will respond positively.

But they don't.

On the surface there can be many reasons for this, but they all boil down primarily to one reason: Spiritual blindness. How else can we account for this refusal to accept eternal life and peace with God and instead take a chance on sure destruction? Even if one is entangled in another religious belief, that belief does not offer fully and freely what is offered in Christianity.

"...but the gift of God is eternal life in Christ Jesus our Lord" (Rom. 6:23).

Did you notice that word "gift?" A gift is something that is given to you, something you need not pay for. To accept it calls for nothing more than reaching out your hand and taking it. You don't have to work for it; you don't have to promise to be good or else you won't get it; you don't have to be afraid of someone else laying claim to it. It's yours free and clear.

You take it and say thank you.

If someone came up to you, handed you the keys to a brand new car, and said, "See that new Buick over there?

It's a gift I bought for you. It's all yours," and you said in response, "I don't want it," or "I don't want to be indebted to you," everyone would think you were crazy. What fool would pass up getting a brand new Buick for nothing?

Or if you said, "I don't believe you," that would be just as weird, especially if that someone had a solid reputation for doing good things for those he loved. You would be dumb to not at least check out the offer. You would also have to be blind to not see its potential value.

In the same sense one has to be spiritually blind to not see, or at least investigate, the value of the gospel message. A capsule version of that message could be, "For all have sinned and fall short of the glory of God, being justified freely by His grace through the redemption that is in Christ Jesus" (Rom. 3:23,24).

Any sinner who does not at least look into the overall meaning of these words will have no one to blame but himself on judgment day.

This blindness can be traced back to the sin of our original parents. It is part of the carnal nature all men are now born with. In Eph. 4:18 men are described as being ignorant and having an understanding that is darkened, caused by the hardness of their hearts. They want nothing to do with spiritual matters.

We see this every day, especially at our place of work. Men will joke about committing adultery, or stealing from the company or government, or getting drunk. Many curse with no thought of misusing the Lord's name. If someone should mention in a serious manner that all this is sin he will immediately be laughed at and labeled a religious fruitcake. The average person does not think in terms of sin. It's an irrelevant issue. He attends his church, loves his mother, pays his bills, and doesn't kill anybody. So what's everyone getting excited about?

Spiritually enlightened Christians, however, are excited and/or concerned about what this individual is unfortunately incapable of seeing. They consider him blind and unable to comprehend the simple facts of spiritual truth. He has been blinded by his sin, by Satan, and to some degree (because of his disobedience) by God himself. (cf. Is. 29:10-12). He is also blind to his immediate danger.

God says in Is. 25:7 that the day will come when He will destroy the covering and the veil that is spread over all people and nations. He will destroy that which keeps men in darkness and prevents them from seeing the way of truth.

That day will surely come, but at the moment we live in an age in which spiritual blindness is a fact of life with which we must deal. It is an unseen negative force that counters the Christian's every move to bring the light of the gospel to those living in darkness. With regard to personal evangelism, ours is a spiritual battle and our enemies are the rulers of the darkness of this age (Eph. 6:12), the very ones who sow confusion and blindness.

Sin corrupts. We see the physical results of sin in the fact that we all suffer various diseases and eventually die. Even creation has been affected by sin (Rom. 8:21). On the spiritual side our nature has been corrupted, our inclinations perverted, and we have become alienated from the life of God. Most people are unaware of this—and that is the maximum spiritual blindness!

The Christian message is clear to those who believe, it is veiled to those who are perishing. Satan, who has been called the god of this age, has blinded the minds of those who do not believe (2nd Cor. 4:3,4), which makes evangelizing difficult, and at times very frustrating. How do we bring light to those who cannot see? Is this an impossible situation?

Yes and no. Some people, by their continuous rejection of God's truth, have placed themselves past the point of no return. They reach the point where they step over the final line, and when that happens God blinds them for good that they might never see. Now they cannot believe because they would not believe—and they are in big trouble!

All this is aptly described in John 12:39,40 where at first glance it seems that God might be acting unfairly. But this is a spiritual judgment that only ratified the decisions previously made. John quotes Isaiah when he says:

"He has blinded their eyes and hardened their hearts, lest they should see with their eyes, Lest they should understand with their hearts and turn, So that I should heal them" (vs. 40).

Some people are now impossible to reach with the gospel. But fortunately the great mass of humanity has not reached that point. There are millions who walk in spiritual darkness, but who are still capable of responding to the light of the gospel message.

Christianity has never been based on "Understand and then you will believe," but rather on, "Believe and then you will understand." Not, "See and then you will know," but instead, "Know Him and then you will see."

A veil of spiritual darkness lies over the heart of every sinner. He is oblivious to the righteousness of God, knowing only that some form of religion might be good in case when he dies there just might be someone out there after all. Religion for the average unregenerate sinner is a form of fire insurance. There's probably no Hell, but just in case.... And God will definitely be pleased with every little bit of religion thrown his way. I mean, no one ever went to Hell because of too much religion. Right...?

Sorry, wrong!

A minority will believe the truth. The majority never has. The Holy Spirit will perform a work of grace in the hearts of those who respond to the call. But that call must be based on the biblical message, the sharp, narrow presentation of the gospel truth as defined in 1st Cor. 15:1-4, and not some hodgepodge of Christian ethics from the Sermon On The Mount or the writings of authors who confuse the issue by using the Bible to teach how to conquer everything from depression to a faulty marriage, and in the process present Christianity as a system of belief designed to make this present life happier for all who follow their advice.

The Bible says faith comes by hearing, and that means hearing the Word of God, and not the lifestyle lectures of preachers who spend more time giving out inspiration than information. Keep one thing in mind. Christianity is an "information oriented" religion. Its central thrust is information. When a preacher steps into a pulpit he is supposed to give out information that the listeners can digest and make part of their thought process. Ours is not a religion based on a ceremony, or a list of rules, or even a particular lifestyle centered on love. Its centerpiece is information! As one fundamentalist preacher put it:

"Preaching is to the church what food is to the supermarket. It's the reason you go there."

The Apostle Paul writes that God in due time manifested His word through *preaching* which was committed to him (Titus 1:3). Preaching is the name of the game, because that's where the action is.

Even though the world walks in spiritual darkness, we know from the Bible that the gospel, if presented properly, can enlighten the hearts and minds of those who are willing to believe.

But how many are willing to see and believe? The great mass of men are described by the Bible as rebellious, lost, and blind, members of a world system opposed to the holy standards of a righteous God. Their understanding has been darkened and they are not in the best of positions.

In fact they are all screwed up!

Doesn't this describe a large percentage of the people we run into? Look around. Read your newspaper, watch your TV, and admit that most of what you see and hear is alien to the life of God. There is a constant and increasing rebellion against any form of godliness that tries to make an appearance, no matter how innocent. In fact it now borders on plain fanaticism with people opposing simple prayers at public events, the Ten Commandments being displayed in a public building, and the slightest mention of God outside the walls of a church.

Why? Because men are blind to the love of God and will not have Him rule over them. The kings and rulers of the earth take counsel together against the Lord and His anointed, saying, "Let us break Their bonds in pieces, and cast away Their cords from us" (Ps. 2:2,3).

This is spiritual blindness activated. It is suicidal in nature, and a mentality steering those who possess it straight into the pit of Hell.

If you cannot see the truth of the Christian faith it is proof that you will perish. The Bible, assuming it is true, says so.

"Yeah, well who says we have to see everything the way you see it?"

Like it or not, the Word of God says that. I'm not inventing what I am saying here. This is fact. There is no scriptural alternative. I'll admit that if the Bible is wrong then I'm wrong. If you can prove from the Bible that what I'm saying is wrong then stand up and let's hear it. I'll listen.

Those who cannot see this, or can see it and still refuse it entry into their lives, and often fight against it—you are lost! Finis, sayonara, arrivederci, and good luck to you.

Cruel? Unloving? This is not the way a Christian should talk…?

I beg your pardon, but unless you're addressing the Ladies Aid Society this is only one example how a Christian should press his point of view. We are dealing here with matters of eternal significance! This is no time for pussyfooting around the issue. Remember, if all this is really true then many people you know are heading for disaster. Wouldn't you want someone to warn you if you were heading for disaster?

As God said, "When I say to the wicked, 'You shall surely die,' and you give him no warning, nor speak to warn the wicked from his wicked way, to save his life, that same wicked man shall die in his iniquity, but his blood I will require at your hand" (Ez. 3:18).

Any Christian with something on the ball will warn you immediately of your peril. That is his responsibility. If you are converted you will understand this, and only then will you be able to understand other spiritual matters. The veil will fall from your eyes (2nd Cor. 3:16) enabling you to comprehend both the mechanics and blessings of the Christian faith. You will no longer be the "natural man" of 1st Cor. 2:14, of whom it is said, "But the natural man does not receive the things of the Spirit of God, for they are foolishness to him; nor can he know them, because they are spiritually discerned."

Spiritual blindness does exist. But it can be penetrated with use of the right light, and that light is the preaching of Christ and Him crucified (cf. 1st Cor. 2:2).

"I am the light of the world. He who follows Me shall not walk in darkness, but have the light of life" (John 8:12). The light is there for all who will make a conscious decision to believe on and receive Christ as their savior.

WHO KILLED JESUS CHRIST?

This question seems to arise almost every year, usually during the Easter season. And more often than not, it is asked and then answered by those who seemingly know nothing about the Bible.

"Who killed Jesus Christ?" must be answered, according to them, in a way that will offend no one except possibly those who revere the name and teaching of this Jesus.

But in order to sell this package the seller has to be manipulative to the extreme. He must first deny the literal truth of the four gospels (which he evidently reads with blinders) and be poised to hurl guilt and the charge of anti-Semitism at those who insist upon taking the historical facts of the gospel for what they are--fact. And he must present his position as the one possessing the compassionate and therefore more Christian viewpoint.

Many "know-nothings" who write for the secular press and publications (and unfortunately some who write for religious publications) claim that (1) Jesus was killed by the Roman authorities, or (2) that He was killed by all of us (figuratively, of course).

We cannot, under pain of being politically incorrect, or appearing anti-Semitic, or un-American, or whatever, say that Jesus was killed by the Jews, or more correctly, by the Jewish religious authorities of that day. We cannot say that because, according to one liberal minister, "Christian leaders have based their blame of Jews as the killers of Christ on New Testament passages and in the process aided and abetted anti-Semitism." The same writer adds, "It is time to speak openly and truthfully about Christian scriptural culpability for both the origins and continuation of anti-Semitism."

Of course if we followed this line of reasoning it would be necessary to junk the whole Bible because it does not line up with accepted twenty-first century American thinking, which to some people is evidently of higher quality than that found in the inspired writings.

But twenty-first century American thinking is not the fount of all truth. What is right and fair, what is equal, what is not discriminatory, has, in recent years, taken on the status of a civil religion. Our society seems overly sensitive about discrimination as if its very existence constituted some kind of national disease.

However no one has the right to gloss over what the Bible plainly teaches just because it might sound discriminatory. When the Bible was written it was not written with the American social ethic in mind. It should not have to be subjected to, or bent to fit, any human tradition, however fine that tradition might be.

When we consider the question of who killed Jesus Christ an immediate uneasiness is created because of the subject's sensitivity, and because there are always those who are quick to hurl the charge of anti-Semitism at anyone who mentions anything about Jews that could possibly be interpreted negatively. So from religious leaders the response to the question as to who killed Jesus Christ is usually a bland, "We all did."

Since we are all sinners, and since Jesus died to save sinners, that reply sounds very fair, and we might add, very American, as it places the blame on everyone equally. And in a very roundabout way (and you really have to stretch this) it could be (in an abstract fashion) theologically correct.

But literally it is just not true! An honest reading of the gospels reveals that Jesus was not killed by "all of us" but by the Jewish religious leaders of that time. Matt. 26:59 says, "Now the chief priests, the elders, and all the council sought false testimony against Jesus to put Him to death."

Why did they want to do this? The answer is best explained in John 5:18 where it is written, "Therefore the Jews sought all the more to kill Him, because He not only broke the Sabbath, but also said that God was His father, making Himself equal with God."

That reads simple enough. Yet we have a columnist for a major Boston newspaper claiming that the idea of the Jews being responsible for the death of Christ is "the longest lie." But how can this be a lie if it lines up perfectly with biblical teaching?

It was Jesus' claim to divinity that Jewish leaders would not tolerate. They were determined that for this Jesus should die, and when they saw the possibility that He might escape this fate by being released instead of Barabbas they took immediate action. "Meanwhile, the chief priests and elders convinced the crowd that they should ask for Barabbas and destroy Jesus" (Matt. 27:20).

There is no other way to answer the question "Who killed Jesus Christ?" than to reply, "The Jewish religious leaders in Jerusalem." Hear their own testimony.

"Therefore, when the chief priests and officers saw Him they cried out, saying, 'Crucify Him, crucify Him!'" Pilate said to them, "You take Him and crucify Him, for I find no fault in Him."

The Jews answered him, "We have a law, and according to our law He ought to die, because He made himself the Son of God' (John 19:6,7).

Yet in spite of this clear biblical evidence we still hear talking heads on TV and in other media saying, "You cannot blame the Jews for the death of Jesus, as it was the Romans who actually killed Him."

This is ridiculous! To these "politically correct" people, what sounds acceptable to our society must now take precedence over historical fact. This kind of twisted thinking could lead some to rewriting other parts of the Bible they may find socially objectionable. History was constantly being rewritten in communist controlled nations. We should not be rewriting history in America—least of all God's history.

Freedom of expression and our intense desire to root out all forms of bigotry and discrimination are worthy goals. But the facts of the Bible should prevail, and all Christians should acknowledge them. Burying biblical truth for the sake of "the American way of looking at things" should not be condoned. Placing the blame on Pilate and his Roman soldiers just doesn't wash. If A hires B to kill C, isn't A just as guilty of the murder as B, if not more so?

Pilate wanted nothing to do with this matter. Didn't he wash his hands before the crowd (Matt. 27:24) absolving himself of any guilt?

But the Jews were not concerned with guilt. In fact in their zeal to see Jesus dead they welcomed it. They cried out, "His blood be on us and on our children" (vs. 25).

And so it has been for the past 2000 years. During that time what people have suffered as much as the Jews? What people have been so persecuted? What other people have had millions murdered in insane genocidal programs? What people have constantly been made the scapegoat for many of the world's problems?

To have compassion for the Jews of this present time should be the natural inclination of any true Christian. Christians do not hate the Jews because of what their ancestors did 2000 years ago. When Hitler murdered millions of Jews during World War 2, he did not do so out of anger at the Jews killing Christ. When Arabs and Palestinians fight against Israel they do not do so for New Testament reasons. Hitler had his agenda and the present day Arabs have theirs, and neither has anything to do with the death of Jesus Christ.

Anti-Semitism is one of the great evils of our time. It can infect different societies for different reasons. But the least of all reasons is theological. Catholics and Protestants who take their faith seriously are, ironically, among the strongest supporters of the state of Israel and of the rights and freedoms of their Jewish neighbors. It is not necessary to rewrite their Bibles for them, or to reinterpret their theology, in order to have them think and believe as intelligent Christians. They already know how to do this.

It is the talking heads on TV and the know-nothing newspaper writers who need a course in getting their facts straight, and then learning how to live with them.

Consider this: In Acts 7 Stephen was speaking to the Jewish high priest and the Jewish council. Near the end of his speech (vs. 52) he said the Jews were the murderers and betrayers of Jesus Christ.

So they killed Stephen also.

Could the Bible make it any more explicit?

Jesus Christ was murdered by a Jewish inspired street mob, and there is no way you can get around that fact! Acknowledging this historical fact does not mean you are anti-Semitic. What it does mean is that you can understand simple English. If the Bible teaches something very plainly, then accept it the way it is written. If it is really true the way it is written, who are you to mess with it? If we allow people to change the answer to this particular question to something that might have more social appeal for some, then we are opening the door to all kinds of shenanigans.

What will be changed or explained away next…?

WHAT ABOUT CAPITAL PUNISHMENT?

At one time theology was considered the queen of the sciences, and there were those who held that every question was ultimately a theological question. But in this present time theology and biblical revelation are no longer considered appropriate guides for the affairs of mankind. We now live in an age of "social enlightenment," an age of positive and scientific thinking that has progressed from the barbarism of the past. We have moved (or so we are told) to a more modern understanding of human nature and behavioral patterns. A murderer, for example, is no longer always looked upon as someone who broke the moral law of God, but as an unfortunate individual whom society has failed, and who, with the help of that society, should be rehabilitated and not punished.

But if the Bible is really true, then this kind of thinking is clearly off base. Capital punishment for the capital crime is the cornerstone of the penal code of western civilization. And it is not cruel and unusual, as some critics claim. Men have been executed for murder and other crimes for thousands of years, so there is nothing unusual about this. And the idea that this is cruel...all punishment contains an element of cruelty. It has to by its very nature, or else it is not punishment. Doing something "bad" to the bad guy is part of the deal. It's payback time.

The late civil rights leader, Dr. Martin Luther King, Jr., wrote in 1957: "Capital punishment is against the best judgment of modern criminology and above all, against the highest expression of love in the nature of God."

Dr. King, on this particular issue, didn't know what he was talking about. His thinking, no doubt, was influenced by the fact that a disproportionate number of those on death row are black. But that fact by itself should not determine the right or wrong of capital punishment.

Abolitionists also claim that too often death sentences are sought not based on the severity of the crime, but on the ambitions of prosecutors and elected judges hoping to curry favor with voters, and that these get-tough positions fly in the face of evidence that the death penalty does not deter murder.

But one must ask what deterrence has to do with the issue. There is no evidence that placing bank robbers in jail deters bank robberies. Does this mean we should no longer put bank robbers in jail?

Dr. King and others should have known that the concept of capital punishment originated with the greatest humanitarian of all—God himself. If one examines the subject in depth he will find it is God who is the author of capital punishment; it is God who decreed that human life is so valuable that the maximum penalty must be paid by those who would destroy it, and it is God who gave us the standards by which we judge those who have committed the supreme crime against humanity.

The Bible says very clearly, "Whoever kills a person, the murderer shall be put to death on the testimony of witnesses...moreover, you shall take no ransom for the life of a murderer who is guilty of death" (Num. 35:30,31), thus making absurd the cry of so-called humanitarians that only God has the right to take human life. The fact that God has delegated to man the power to kill through the authority of human government is clear beyond dispute.

Yet we hear the American Catholic bishops speaking out against capital punishment as wrong and against the teaching of the church. But one must ask, Why is the teaching of the church different from the clear teaching of the Bible? Both cannot be right. If the Bible is really true, the Catholic bishops should be criticized strongly for teaching that which is wrong and without biblical foundation.

The abolitionists claim that capital punishment is not a deterrent, that there is no proof that the execution of murderers is an effective warning to potential murderers.

But this is an empty argument. There is no possible way to determine how many murders have not been committed by those who wanted to commit the act but did not for fear of possible execution. Furthermore, whether or not it is a deterrent is beside the point. God did not demand that murderers be executed as examples to others as much as they were to be executed because that is what His justice demanded. Executing murderers is not undertaken for social or economic reasons; it is undertaken for moral reasons. The only valid question is, Does the supreme crime deserve the supreme penalty? Those who make deterrence the main issue miss the basic point of the whole argument.

We often hear the charge that executing murderers cheapens human life. But actually it is those who would do away with capital punishment who cheapen human life. If a man is murdered and his killer spends 30 years in prison for the crime, then in effect the state is saying the victim's life was only worth 30 years of the killer's life. If the killer spends only 5 years in prison for the crime, the state is then saying that the victim's life was worth only 5 years of the killer's life. If the killer is not punished at all, then the state is saying the victim's life was worthless.

However, if the killer had to pay for the crime with his own life, then the state would be exacting from him the maximum penalty, and would in effect be placing the highest possible value on the victim's life.

If God's justice is to mean anything then He must punish the breaking of His moral law. And if God's laws are the prototype of all earthly law (as the Bible indicates they should be), then by what right should the state and its citizens disregard the penalties that God has commanded and in effect say they do not take His commandments seriously? That state could be heading for big trouble, as this is the beginning of the breakdown of law and order.

The Catechism of the Catholic Church (2267) says, "If bloodless means are sufficient to defend human lives against an aggressor…public authority should limit itself to such means, because they better correspond to the concrete conditions of the common good and are more in conformity to the dignity of the human person."
But if the Bible is really true this makes no sense. Society has no business worrying about the dignity of a cold-blooded killer. By his actions the murderer has forfeited his right to the dignity and respect of his peers.
Justice, in the biblical sense of the word, is the administering of punishment without respect of persons. It is the balance of guilt or injury with satisfaction and atonement.   It should not be warped by philosophical musings on the dignity of the murderer (a dignity, I might add, that the Bible knows nothing about).

"Yeah, but they could put the guy in jail and he could get rehabilitated."
Don't make me laugh.   Criminals do not get rehabilitated in jail. They get smart (if they have any brains at all) and figure out ways to avoid getting caught again when they get out. If they're really smart they'll figure a life of crime isn't worth the possibility of being slammed into prison again. So they go straight. But this is not the result of a jail program rehabilitating anyone.

It should be obvious that the state does not have the right to forgive, nor the power or ability to reform or rehabilitate criminals. A state whose law operated on the principles of love and forgiveness would invite its own destruction. The state exists to exercise its powers of restraint. Its function is negative. It is the church that was given the positive approach (preaching forgiveness and love). The responsibilities of the two powers are clearly defined.

The state has no more ability to reform a sinner than the church has to apprehend a car thief. When the state abandons its limited function of punishing evil, and takes upon itself the responsibility of reforming criminals, it becomes derelict in its divinely ordained duty and can only end up doing neither effectively.

Just think: If the state had the ability to reform murderers, rapists, and assorted gangsters, wouldn't a man be better off taking his family to jail on Sundays instead of church? If the state can straighten out hardened criminals, just think what it could do with members of your family who hadn't yet reached that stage?

"Where is your high school Sunday school class today, Mrs. Brown?"

"Oh, they went to the state penitentiary today instead. It seems they have a better program that gets real good results."

Yeah, sure. What do they do, yell BE GOOD, BE GOOD, into your ears 12 hours every day? Or do they inject you with Nice Guy serum? How does someone get rehabilitated in jail? Does anyone really know…?

The Bible says, "Therefore, if anyone is in Christ he is a new creation; old things have passed away; behold, all things have become new" (2nd Cor. 5:17). That is what you call real rehabilitation, and that takes place under the preaching of the gospel in a church, and not hanging around with a bunch of thugs in the state pen. (Although it must be noted that there are gospel ministries in many prisons that do produce fruit.)

As St. Augustine wrote, "The state, far from being an instrument of human emancipation from sin and the perfectibility of criminals, is merely a strait jacket for human sinfulness, to be justified at best as a divinely appointed means of restraining sin, while the church gets on with the business of mediating to mankind the grace and love of God which alone can redeem and reform men of their sins."

Capital punishment is that which the murderer has brought upon himself by his actions. According to the Bible (Deut. 17:7) it was undertaken to purge evil from among the people, and not to teach potential murderers a lesson (although that was a secondary effect).

In Num. 35:33 God said, "...for blood defiles the land, and no atonement can be made for the land, for the blood that is shed on it, except by the blood of him who shed it."

That—like it or not—is the biblical view on the subject. If the Bible is true it would make sense for governments to follow its directives on this issue.

God considers murder a socially disruptive act that must be punished, and this is accomplished by the death of the murderer. The advantage which he has unlawfully acquired is taken from him and the injury suffered by society repaired. There is no thought here of reform or rehabilitation. Punishment is meted out as a just dessert for the act, and nothing more.

The abolitionist movement which has grown strong in recent years is obviously not based on moral grounds, regardless of its claim to the contrary. It is propagated mainly by those who feel it is somehow the fault of society that men are evil, and that therefore they should not be held *fully* responsible for their actions.

But again, this is against everything the Bible teaches. God holds every individual responsible for his actions. No one will ever be able to pass off his sin as the fault of others or his environment.

We have a choice. Shall we be governed by laws whose origins are found in the teachings of a moral and righteous God, or shall we be governed by the philosophies of men whose basic misconception of human nature lead them to believe that through the proper regulation of the social order man can attain perfection independent of the redeeming grace of God?

Look around you. Read the papers. Watch the TV news. The whole world is turning into a violent cartoon. In your own defense would you rather be governed by the laws of God, or by the theories of some sequestered whacked out academics?

If the Bible is really true, you'll be a lot safer being guided by its precepts.

EVOLUTION AND COMMON SENSE

If the Bible is really true, then the theory of evolution has to be one of the most bizarre and idiotic assumptions ever foisted upon mankind. In fact, why not go a step further. If the Bible is *not* true, evolution would still be one of the most bizarre and idiotic assumptions ever foisted upon mankind for the simple reason that organic evolution is (according to many knowledgeable people) a scientific impossibility.

Yet this theory has heavily influenced our society for the past 100 years, not in the average home, but in our educational institutions. It has been bandied about as fact by those devoted to this viewpoint, and by those who consider any other alternative to be equivalent with backwoods religious fundamentalism.

But the idea that evolution is an established fact of science is false. It is the "belief" of some segments of the scientific community, and nothing more. The very essence of science is based on observation and experimentation, and since it is impossible to observe or conduct an experiment on the origin of life, the theory must be believed strictly on faith. In the final analysis those who accept evolution are no different from those who accept the creation story as described in the Bible.

Dr. George Wald, winner of the 1967 Nobel Peace Prize, once wrote, "When it comes to the origin of life on this earth, there are only two possibilities: creation or spontaneous generation. There is no third way. Spontaneous generation was disproved 100 years ago, but that leads us to only one other conclusion, that of supernatural creation.

"We cannot accept that on philosophical grounds; therefore we chose to believe the impossible, that life arose spontaneously by chance."

That says volumes! Evolutionists do not believe in evolution because it is a proven fact. They believe in evolution because the only other alternative they find unacceptable. So since evolution <u>must</u> be true—then it is true!

Before going any further it might be good, just for a moment, to use some good old fashioned common sense. Do you have any idea how many different living organisms there are on this planet? Between all the plants and animals and insects and fish and people and some things we probably don't even know about yet, it must run into the hundreds of thousands, or even millions, and that's just a wild guess. Even if we're off by half a million, the point here is that we are being asked to believe that one day one something-or-other had two kids, and one was an animal and one was a vegetable. If this thing had only one kid then we would have all been animals or vegetables. If we were all animals there would have been no vegetation to eat. If we turned out all vegetables there wouldn't have been any conscious life on this planet.

So it's a good thing that great, great, great (and add a few zillion more "greats" here) grandmother had twins the first time she conceived. (Although no one knows how she went about conceiving anything, as there was no other living thing in the neighborhood at the time; or how she split in half, or whatever…)

But none of this bothers the evolutionist. All life came about by chance and evolved into thousands (millions?) of different creatures because there is no other logical way to explain it.

Okay, but where is the proof, evidence, whatever…? If this is true, then shouldn't the earth be filled with the remains of all these creatures in their partially evolved state?

Shouldn't we be finding the remains of half of this and half of that? Is it asking too much to see the remains of a gorilla with maybe human feet, or of a whatever-it-was that had already evolved into half a giraffe? I mean, just where are all these mutations that changed and evolved into all these things? Their fossils must be somewhere…?

And please, never mind all this foolishness about finding a finger bone somewhere and from this concluding that the owner was 5'1" tall, that he was a farmer, that his wife was a redhead who ran off with the stone mason next door, and that he finally killed himself by jumping off a cliff because the finger is bent in a way that could only be caused by falling from a great height.

This makes for a good TV documentary, and very good entertainment, but hardly good science. It's almost as funny as the scientist who amazes the world with the finding of a new skull, and from the shape of the skull decides what this guy ate, what he did for a living, and the extent of his intelligence. And of course how many millions of years ago he lived.

The funny thing is, you can walk down the street of any city in this country and within five minutes find people with heads shaped very different from one other. Some people have very small and round heads, others elongated heads; some have high foreheads, others low foreheads, and some have square heads. And yet they are all living within the same time period. So to find a piece of skull somewhere and because of its shape decide that the owner lived within the "whatever" period, and that he evolved from a guy whose jawbones were much thicker, etc., is laughable. Better yet, it's pure fantasy. But as long as it makes for good entertainment, and the ones who discovered it get more research money, what real difference does it make?

Such is our world at the present time. People believe not what has been proved, but what seems more comfortable and acceptable.

Consider this: You are reading this page with the use of your two eyes. Most animals also have two eyes. With some exceptions this is also true for most insects, and probably true for most fish. Two eyes in the middle of the head seems to be the norm.

But why? If eyes evolved by chance, on thousands of people, animals, and fish, wouldn't the occasional roll of the dice come up with maybe something developing a big eye in the middle of its stomach, or on the top of its head, or three of them on the right thigh? Once in a while, anyway…?

Why not? Imagine zebras with a big eye stuck between their front legs. They could see the grass better and would not always have to be stretching down looking for good grazing. Or how about a mouse with two eyes in front and two eyes in the back of his head so he can see who might be sneaking up on him? And why do most fish seem to have two eyes in the front of their heads just like we do? Could this be a clue that the human race evolved from a family of mutant codfish? Or maybe mutant rattlesnakes? Don't rattlesnakes have two eyes in the front of their heads like we do? Sounds good to me, don't you think…?

Or how about the $64 question: How did eyes evolve in the first place, and was there once a time when no living creature had eyes and everyone was walking around bumping into trees and walking off cliffs and maybe starving because they couldn't find any food?

Even the most rabid evolutionist would have to admit that the first living "thing" did not possess two eyes with 20/20 vision. The first living thing was blind as a bat at high noon. But somehow he found something to eat. He could not have eaten anyone else because there was no one else. So what did he eat? Who knows? Evolutionists do not worry about things like that. Let's just say his first meal was a drink of water and let it go at that. He did not have to see water as he was probably floating in it at the time.

Somehow (and this is one big "somehow") our little friend's kids took on one or two new characteristics, which is really a tremendous feat since it is impossible to pass off to offspring characteristics the parents do not have.

Example: If you and your spouse have a child you can rest assured that when he is ten years old he will not begin growing blue feathers on his arms or a beak on his mouth. It's just not going to happen.

Why not? Because you don't have the ability to do that. So he won't either. It's not in your genetic code. This code is universal and applies to all species.

Yet the first "thing," when multiplying (How did he or she do that?) began passing on these tremendous abilities, one of which had to be the beginning piece of the ability to see. Some lucky (whatever it was by that time) was born with the ability to begin the step-by-step evolution of the eyeball.

But why?

"Well nature decided that---"

Hold it! Don't give me that nature decided stuff again. Nature can't decide anything because it can't think. Nature does not have brains or intelligence and is incapable of deciding anything.

The truth of the matter is, there was no good reason for the evolution of eyesight anymore than there was a reason for the evolution of anything else. It just "fortunately" happened (according to the theory of evolution).

Now began the accidental birth of what we know as the eyeball, which, by the way, is characterized by a staggering complexity. It possesses automatic focusing, automatic aperture adjustment, and can see during both day and night—and does it all in living color! No doubt this is one of the greatest accidents in history.

But there's more. This eyeball also contains muscles that control its movements, veins and arteries that feed it necessary blood, and an actual lens through which the light rays pass.

Obviously this marvelous mechanism did not evolve overnight. Being so intricate it must have taken many years.

And keep in mind that this mechanism would be totally useless until completed. So what we have is something being built totally by accident and heading for a grand finale of perfection. (I don't think so.) One little glitch along the way and we have no eyes and most likely no way of surviving. We would have a planet full of people staggering around crashing into each other, unable to grow or catch food, unable to read and advance their civilization, and who would probably not survive for too long, if at all.

But lucky for us the accident of "eyeball making" fell into place. The optic nerve that supplies the retina and conducts visual stimuli to the brain just "happened" to develop in the right spot; the pupil of the eye ended up right in front where it will do the most good; and the lacrimal gland formed to secrete clear saline fluid (tears) that is diffused between the eyes and the eyelids to moisten the parts and facilitate their motion.

Be honest with your own mind and heart. The chances of all this happening quite by accident over thousands or millions of years is so staggering as to be virtually impossible by any sensible standard of measurement.

And then consider this: This same wild accident also took place with squirrels, cats, weasels, sharks, cobras, and everything else that has two eyes in the front of its head. Now what are the chances of all this happening by chance and arriving at the same result, the ability to see?

Don't even try to figure it out.

But then again, maybe it didn't happen quite that way. Maybe eyes evolved in the First Whatever before things branched off. Perhaps one fine day the First Whatever (meaning the first living thing, whatever it was) was crawling along and all the intricacies of its eye finally formed and it began to function. He suddenly says to himself, "Hey, wow, get a load of this. Look at all this neat stuff all over the place that I never saw before."

Let us assume, also, (and there is nothing wrong here with assuming, as evolutionists do it all the time) that the

First Whatever's eye was like a tadpole's eye. When the different species branched off into cats and dogs and monkeys and snakes, etc., why didn't all these creatures end up with tadpole eyes?

"Well each creature has its own eyes to suit its own environment, and---"
Whoa, wait a minute here. What you are now saying is that this whole improbable process has to begin all over again to suit individual creatures? You can't be serious!

A snake's eye is different from a human eye, and a human eye is different from a cat's eye, and so on down the line. So we are not really dealing with one eye after all, but with many kinds of eyes. Which means that the machinery for the tadpole eyeball—unaided by any outside source—for some strange reason began changing to fit various situations? (I don't think so.)
But let's say it changed (evolved). What made it change? How did the cat's eye know that it would have to change to see better at night? And since this is all random happenstance anyway, aren't the chances of something screwing up while trying to change (evolve) better than even? And doesn't that mean that close to half of all creatures should have then ended up blind? In fact maybe even the majority? I mean, it doesn't take much to screw up an eyeball.
Consider this: Let's find an empty lot and fill it with glass, pieces of rubber, leather, metal, nuts, bolts, gears, plastic, etc. We throw this stuff into one big pile. Then once every week we have an earthquake that measures 6 on the Richter scale. If you believe that in one or two billion years all these earthquakes will turn this pile of material into a brand new Cadillac all ready to drive, then you can believe that your eyeball sprouted from who-knows-what into what it is today. You can become a member of Evolutionists Anonymous.

Some things to keep in mind.

The propaganda barrage from those who support the theory of evolution goes on without letup. They follow the belief that "The more you say something, the more it becomes fact." And that if you say it long enough and loud enough it becomes incontrovertible fact.

(Nazi propagandists followed the same program.)

One classic example is the idea that species produce mutations that then develop into new species. A legitimate mutation is an inherited physical or biochemical change in genetic material.

But scientists will be quick to acknowledge that the great majority of mutations in any living thing are degenerative in nature. They are not a step up, but a step down, and they more often than not die out, as they are not able to survive. Furthermore, it has not yet been shown experimentally that mutations can produce new structures or new organs.

Limited changes have been observed in some species, but that does not mean that after millions of years these species evolved into different creatures entirely. When an evolutionist says that is exactly what happened, he should offer some proof. But there is no proof because no one was there to observe and record what happened. It is just assumed that this took place. This assumption is what makes evolution only a theory and not a fact.

Yet there are those who continue advancing the belief that a tiny percent of mutations provided new design information that eventually led to Tyrannosaurus Rex or some other dinosaur evolving into a pigeon.

Yes, you read that right. The theory has been presented that the scales of reptiles eventually evolved into feathers and that many of these reptiles and dinosaurs became birds.

Anyone who believes that will believe anything!

An added problem for the evolutionist is the fact that reptile lungs contain millions of tiny air sacs, but bird lungs have tubes and not sacs. In the process of evolving from one into the other we would have creatures whose lungs function on both air sacs and tubes.

Now how does that work?

Mathematically speaking, the concept that life arose spontaneously millions (or billions) of years ago, and evolved into what you see now on the main street of your town or city, is so improbable it literally defies explanation. The idea that life originated and developed purely by chance and aimless natural process is comparable to the probability of a monkey sitting down and typing out a perfect unabridged dictionary of the English language. In order to do this the monkey would have to select about 35 million letters in their proper sequence.

Fat chance!

And yet on TV nature programs the bombardment goes on without ceasing, the narrator's voice describing the evolutionary process as if he were describing something as simple as a road map. There is no question that this did not happen; there is no possibility of an alternative point of view; there is no need for one anyway…so they say.

They say evolution takes a long time. A very, very, very long time. That is why evolutionists are always throwing around figures like "350 million years ago…" and other wild numbers as if the difference between 350 million years and 348 million years was practically meaningless. But can you even imagine one million years by our time standard?

And then we have those who throw out "Billions of years ago…" which stretches our imagination to its limits and is used to completely nullify our ability to intelligently understand the subject matter. These scientists throw out numbers and years with abandon to the point of becoming nonsensical.

However, other scientists have shown that even if the earth was once in a molten state, from the first moments of its cooling, until it reached its present temperature, that time would not have exceeded 45 million years. (So what's with all the billions…?)

But 45 million years is not enough time for an amoeba to evolve into the guy next door, so these little facts are conveniently ignored, as are hundreds of other little facts that intrude upon this theory. Like the following:

The genetic information contained in each cell of your body has a rough equivalence to a library of thousands of volumes. The probability that mutations created this vast amount of information is realistically nonexistent.

Assuming that proteins evolved from nothing—against almost impossible odds—there is no reason to believe that by themselves they could form a membrane-encased, self-producing, living cell. No scientist has ever shown how this tremendous jump in complexity could have occurred.

There is no proof of any mutation producing a new form of life that has greater complexity and viability than its ancestors. There has never existed a mutant that has been discovered crossing the line into another species.

Yet all this is essential to the theory of evolution.

But it never happened!

"Yeah, but it had to have happened somewhere along the line or things would not have evolved."

But to our knowledge it didn't happen. And from what we know about genetic codes, and chromosomes, and DNA, etc., it can't happen!

"Yeah, but---"

Forget it, pal. You are asking me to believe the impossible, and to top it off you are asking me to believe that believing the impossible is scientific. You'll have to do better than that.

There are some who will insist that it's within the realm of possibility that when the conditions were just right a form of life could have arisen from nonliving molecules and amino acids. They will insist that we can't be one hundred percent sure that this did not happen.

Okay, let's play that one out just for the sake of discussion. What is the simplest form of life, a virus or some kind of bacteria? Whatever it is it had to be able to reproduce in order to support your theory.

Let's takc the virus. In order for this guy to reproduce he has to invade a living cell and attack the protein molecules in order to duplicate its composition. This guy is a parasite, and he lives by invading and then destroying a living cell in order to reproduce his kind.

The living cell is his food. Remember a little way back when we discussed the first living thing and asked what it ate? We settled for a glass of water to avoid getting all tangled up in the unknown. But now we have to get a bit more specific. Here we have this virus guy eating a living cell—which then means he was not the first living thing! If he was he would have starved to death and been unable to reproduce.

The same can be said if the first living thing was some kind of bacteria, the smallest single cell organism we have. He is a cell of protoplasm surrounded by a membrane. In his first conscious moment he is going to ask, "Okay, what's for lunch?"

Depending upon the kind of bacteria he is (some eat dead animal or vegetable matter, and others eat only live animal or vegetable matter), he has to immediately go hunting.

But hunting for what? If he is the first living thing to come along, then there was not at that time any animal or vegetable matter on which to feed. He too then starves to death. And so ends the saga of what could have become the human race.

When God said, "Let us make man in our image, according to our likeness…" (Gen. 1:26), He was not talking about some unthinking microscopic "thing" floating in a mud puddle. He was talking about making someone who is very similar to you. And according to the Bible that is exactly what He did.

If you do not believe that, and honestly think that you evolved haphazardly from some piece of sludge, which means that you have no soul or sin, and therefore no accountability to God, then according to the Bible—you could be in big trouble!

WAS THERE REALLY A GREAT FLOOD?

If the Bible is really true, then some time within the past 12 to 15 thousand years (give or take a few here or there), the earth suffered a catastrophic flood that covered the highest mountains of that time and killed all land creatures except those in Noah's famous ark.

This is hard to believe for the simple reason that our minds cannot fully comprehend such an event. Water a mile or so deep…or even deeper…everywhere, and on the surface floating carcasses of men and animals from every corner of the planet?

Unbelievable! This would rank as the greatest natural disaster of all time. Such death and destruction had never been seen before, and has not been witnessed since.

But did it really happen?

According to the biblical writers, and Jesus Christ, it did. Every chapter from Gen. 1 through 11 is referred to somewhere in the New Testament (the flood took place in the 7th chapter) as authoritative, meaning that if they took these things as fact, they must have also taken the flood account as fact.

Also, every New Testament writer refers at least once to something in Gen. 1-11. They were quoting, as they believed, from authority. If the flood did not take place, then what these writers had to say (concerning the events of Gen. 1-11) is of little value, or simply just not true.

Since we have no eyewitnesses to the event, and no first hand on-the-scene reports, we must rely on either the biblical record, or on traces of earthly evidence.

The biblical record will of course be discounted by those who do not believe the Bible to be literally true. Why should they take what certain New Testament writers said, or even what Jesus said, if they do not take as true what Moses (the author of Genesis) wrote?

So we will ignore for the moment the biblical record, and concentrate instead on the earthly record, and we can begin with this one startling fact:

Every major mountain range on earth contains fossilized sea life.

Why? And how did it get there?

Fish do not climb mountains, and shellfish do not fly through the air. It becomes obvious, then, that at one time these mountains were underwater.

Scattered throughout the world are large caches of animal bones in what are known as "rubble drift in ossiferous fissures." These fissures are great rips in the earth that occur during earthquakes and other disruptions of the earth's surface. The rubble found in these fissures is usually placed there by moving water during these disruptions. Many of these fissures are filled with the bones of animals such as elephants, reindeer, horses, pigs, and oxen. The bodies are not intact or complete, but have been ripped apart and seemingly been thrown together in chaotic fashion.

The Rock of Gibraltar reportedly has bone-filled fissures that run 300 feet deep, and similar deposits can be found on hills of considerable height. In Nebraska there is a hill on which a bone bed was found that contains the remains of thousands of animals. A great flood of water is the only thing that can logically account for this strange phenomenon. Why else would animals that do not usually live together congregate on higher elevations and then die together?

And how else can we account for the thousands of woolly mammoths found buried in the Arctic regions, many of them preserved in upright positions and with food in their mouths?

In the book "Fingerprints Of The Gods" by Graham Hancock (not a religious book), Hancock writes, "About 14,000 years ago some murderous upheaval hit the northern regions of Alaska and Siberia resulting in frozen animals with their flesh still intact." He goes on to tell of mammoth carcasses that are found and then unfrozen to feed sled dogs, and of the smell of rotting meat from the ground when the weather turns unusually warm.

He writes of an Alaskan muck containing twisted parts of animals and trees that are intermingled with ice, peat and moss, and also the remains of bison, horses, wolves, and even lions and bears. Whole herds of them killed by some unexplained catastrophe. Obviously these body piles did not develop by natural means. These animals, trees, and assorted vegetation were all covered with a fine, sifting muck and were then frozen in the ground. What else could have done this except a flood of tremendous proportion accompanied by a radical temperature change?

Let's keep in mind the obvious truth that when animals die they are not given Christian burials by those animals still living. They die above ground and rot, or are eaten by scavengers. Their bones are picked over by birds and other small animals and eventually scattered far and wide.

How then did these thousands (some say hundreds of thousands) of animals in the Arctic region get buried and then frozen? What cataclysmic event caused this? Could it have been anything less than a wall of tremendous flood-water filled with debris of all kinds picked up from the whole of the Northern Hemisphere? How do we account for all this apart from an event of such magnitude that it's almost impossible to imagine? The burial of millions of fossils, fish, land animals and plants, preserved in huge sedimentary deposits, could not have happened by any process we know of today.

Was this flood just one big prolonged rainstorm?

Evidently not. In Gen. 7:11 it says, "…the fountains of the great deep were broken up, and the windows of heaven were opened." This was the beginning of the flood. In Gen. 8:2, at the end of the flood, it says, "The fountains of the deep and the windows of heaven were also stopped…"

Water evidently came from two directions, one being "The fountains of the deep," which means that some of the water feeding this great flood had to have burst forth with extreme violence from beneath the crust of the earth, from subterranean interconnected chambers that held almost as much if not more water that fell from the heavens.

If it did happen this way, it would go far in explaining many of the strange and mysterious formations on this planet, including the great ocean trenches, frozen mammoths, the Grand Canyon, fossil graveyards, major mountain ranges, coal and oil formations, and possibly volcanoes and earthquakes.

The large coal beds and oil fields all over the earth could easily have been created by the effects of the flood. They are usually believed to have been created by the actions of natural forces over millions of years. But it is within the realm of possibility that much if not all of this could have been created at one time by the burial of tremendous quantities of vegetable and animal matter.

It has already been scientifically demonstrated that a cylindrical 2 inch piece of wood can be turned into a (almost) piece of coal by placing it inside a steel tube, adding water, and heating it to 160 degrees centigrade for two weeks. The chemical reaction between the steam and heat causes the *beginning* of the coalification of the piece of wood. So who needs millions of years for the final product?

Where is the evidence that the "fountains of the deep" were broken up? In the 1950s a unique discovery was made: The Mid-Oceanic Ridge. This ridge is a mountain range roughly 40,000 miles long under the seas that wraps itself around the whole earth. It is composed mainly of a rock called basalt that differs from the rock of almost all other mountains. If you were to look at the earth from space, and drain all the ocean waters, the planet would look very much like a baseball with all its stitches showing. These stitches would be the Mid-Oceanic Ridge.

How did this ridge get there, and why is it all under the ocean? Was this the place where the earth split open and allowed the waters to burst forth? The Bible says, "He gathers the waters of the sea together as a heap; He lays up the deep in storehouses" (Ps. 33:7). The water was there, and when it joined the water coming down from above, it was more than enough to cover the entire earth. "And the waters prevailed exceedingly on the earth, and all the high hills under the whole heaven were covered" (Gen. 7:19).

Of course, if the Bible is not true, then we must come up with some other explanation as to how the Grand Canyon was formed, why mammoths were frozen upright in the very act of eating, and what possibly happened to the dinosaurs, among other questions.

The reality of a worldwide flood, however, allows for a credible answer to these questions. The Grand Canyon was obviously carved out when tons of rushing water swept away the softer parts of the earth; the mammoths were frozen when the vapor canopy that covered the earth at that time collapsed and fell in torrents, drowning and then freezing that animals under the Arctic tundra; and the dinosaurs could easily have been destroyed in the flood waters. The few small ones surviving in the ark might have found this new climate not to their liking and died out.

There are some who hold that the flood was not a worldwide flood, that it was only local in scope. But how would you contain water that was higher than the mountains (regardless of how high they might have been at the time) to a local area without it running off sideways? And how would you kill all flesh on earth with only a local flood? And who says that all the hundreds of thousands (or millions) who might have been living on the earth at that time lived in the Middle East? If a certain tribe went about

900 miles to the north did the "local" flood send out tentacles to get them? Did this local flood look like some kind of octopus? Where does the Bible give any indication of this? And why would Noah take two of every animal into the ark to preserve the species if the species could easily reproduce themselves outside the local flood area?

In fact, if the flood was only local, wouldn't it have made more sense to just tell Noah and his family to hop on their camels and move out of the area? That would have been much easier than wasting all those backbreaking years building an ark.

The Bible indicates it was a worldwide flood. The earth shows evidence of a worldwide flood. If the Bible is really true there was a worldwide flood. If this section of the Bible is true, the chances are very good that the rest of the Bible is true.

And if it is, and you are not tuned into all of this…you could be in a very serious condition that needs immediate fixing.

THE GREAT ESCAPE

Our present world is in big trouble. There are screwballs everywhere who now possess nuclear weapons, poison gas, biological weapons, and above all a fanatical hatred for other cultures and religions.

This is a dangerous mix. Let one screwball go over the line and we're going to have one big mess on our hands. We have seen the disaster of the World Trade Center attack on what is now knows as 9-11. Multiply that by ten or more, then picture the same carnage in other major cities of the world…and it's something you don't even want to think about. You would be sitting in front of your TV set spellbound, maybe even trembling (assuming you were one of the initially untouched), wondering if you should jump into your car and head for the hills. In the forefront of your mind would be one basic thought—escape!

In the biblical record there are some who escaped great disasters, and some who did not, and some who will not. Among those in our future who *will not* escape the wrath of God will be the unsaved on *the day of the Lord*. This day is mentioned, among other places, in1st Thess. 5:2-4 where it says, "For you yourselves know perfectly that the day of the Lord so comes as a thief in the night. For when they say 'Peace and safety' then sudden destruction comes upon them, as labor pains upon a pregnant woman. <u>And they shall not escape</u>. But you, brethren, are not in darkness, so that this Day should overtake you as a thief."

If people at that time are saying "Peace and safety" it's evident that they feel secure. There is no immediate threat of attack on the horizon; times are good and life is good. Let the good times roll!

But these people will have no real concept of what is actually going on. They are sons of darkness (vs. 5). They will be blind to the nature of the times (vs. 6). They will be spiritually asleep and it will all go right over their heads.

So when sudden destruction comes they will not escape! It will be too late for them to change their ways, it will be too late to repent. For them the day of grace is over, and now there is no escape!

It will not be like this for the Christian. He will be aware of what is going on in the world (vs. 4), as he is always being told to watch (Matt. 24:42). Christians have the Word of God to guide them; they will have an understanding of things of which the world is unaware. They will (or should) be conscious of the world system's impending doom.

It is interesting to note that one of the opening salvos of New Testament ministry was not the declaration of the love of God, but rather a call to repentance from John the Baptist accompanied by the words, "Brood of vipers! Who warned you to flee from the wrath to come?" (Matt. 3:7).

Already the sense of *escape* was in the air. There was nothing jovial in the ministry of John the Baptist. There was no heralding of good times to come, no message that John had come to share the love of God with anyone.

Instead there was a message of "You'd better straighten out fast—or else!" When he spoke of the coming of Jesus his words were still hard. "And even now the ax is laid to the root of the trees. Therefore every tree which does not bear good fruit is cut down and thrown into the fire" (Matt. 3:10). Jesus is coming to separate the wheat from the chaff (the good from the evil) and then burn the chaff (the wicked) with unquenchable fire (vs. 12).

"That sounds like a tough attitude for someone who calls himself a savior."

Maybe it does. But this is one way that Jesus is described. You can't blot it out just because it makes you nervous.

"How come when I go to church I never hear Jesus being described as someone who might be hard to deal with?"

Ever think that might be because you're attending a church that does not teach the whole counsel of God, a church that first wants to make sure you feel comfortable so you'll come back next week, and that if you die before you come back, well…that's the breaks?

Any way you look at it, the earthly ministry of Jesus Christ was a ministry of judgment upon a sin sick world. He exposed the true nature of men; He drew a sharp line between righteousness and unrighteousness; and He was rigid in his insistence that only through Him could one find God and eternal life. On His cross the world was judged and our sins atoned for—that we might escape the wrath to come (cf. 1st Thess. 1:10).

There are a number of great escapes mentioned in the Bible, the most notable, Noah escaping from the flood, and Lot escaping from Sodom and Gomorrah. In both instances these men were warned ahead of time to prepare and then get out. They were the righteous in a situation gone rotten. With Noah it was a matter of God giving him the plans on how to make his escape. With Lot it was a matter of angels literally taking him by the hand and leading him to safety. Both escaped through the grace of God.

In like manner we can escape wrath through the grace of God that has been provided to us by the redemption that is in Christ Jesus (cf. Rom. 3:24). This is our way of escape, and it is the only way of escape now available. This is the narrow gate mentioned by Jesus in both Matt. 7:13 and Luke 13:24.

There is no other way! The world with all its varied religions, with all its mad religious fanaticism, with all its grand moral pronouncements, with all its media clerics spouting great swelling words of emptiness (2nd Peter 2:18), can provide nothing because it has no base in truth. A Christless society with only a form of godliness is of no value to anyone.

"Watch therefore, and pray always that you may be counted worthy to escape all these things that will come to pass, and to stand before the Son of Man" (Luke 21:36).

Being counted "worthy to escape all these things that will come to pass…" should be the main concern of every person who breathes the air of this life. There is no other issue more important than escaping the wrath of God, and its consequence—*the eternal damnation of your soul!*

Unfortunately most people do not seem to care. They go about their business like those in Noah's day, eating and drinking and giving in marriage, and probably attending the important sporting events of the day, and hustling to make a buck, and making plans for that new house…until the flood came and swept them all away. Even now many listen to the siren song of those who disparage Christianity in any form.

"It's all a racket," they say. "Look at all those priests and ministers getting caught messing around. And how about those phony TV healers always asking poor old women to send them money so they can get cured of their arthritis. Boy, what a scam! Ha, I should have gotten into something like that."

There are phonies everywhere, and there always will be. Turn on your cable TV and watch a religious channel and the fakers practically fall out of the screen onto your living room floor. It's a Christian's job to test what he sees and hears against the Word of God so he can know the con men and not be fooled by their deceiving doctrines (1st John 4:1).

Does recognizing and laughing at these fakers enhance your chances of escaping the judgment of God if you're a non-believer? I wouldn't count on it. You will still get hammered. And to expect others to renounce their beliefs because of a few bad apples makes absolutely no sense. We are all familiar with recent government officials who disgraced their office and their families and who lacked the sense to even be ashamed of their actions. But none of us decided to renounce our citizenship because of this. We did not say the whole country was no good. We did not emigrate to other lands.

Yet when we see fakers who advance into fame and fortune in religious circles, we find those who are eager to condemn the whole Christian movement and everything it ever stood for, even its Founder who was never convicted of any sin. By doing this they eliminate their own chances of escaping the wrath to come. Jesus has provided mankind a way of escape. The invitation to avail oneself of this is called the preaching of the gospel. Ignore it and you will be damned!

The writer asks, "How shall we escape if we neglect so great a salvation, which at the first began to be spoken by the Lord, and was confirmed to us by those who heard Him" (Heb. 2:3).

And the answer is: You won't.

Even if you could prove that 70% of all priests and ministers were pedophiles, thieves, and adulterers, and that some churches were taking in millions with shady investments, you still won't escape, because you are foolishly allowing this stuff to blind you to the only way of salvation that exists. Talk about being dumb.

"Yeah, but everybody knows that churches are filled with hypocrites."

Even if that were true, that fact in itself isn't going to get you off the hook.

The actual escape will take place at the Second Coming of Christ. There is a fiction that Jesus will first come secretly and take believers out of the world. This is known as the pretribulation rapture of the church. The church is taken out of the world, everything goes crazy for 7 years, including the anti-Christ who tries running the show, and then Jesus comes again, only this time in judgment.

But it's not going to happen that way.

"You mean to tell me you think the church is going to be here on earth during the seven years of great tribulation?"

Yes, and the reason I believe that is because there isn't a thing in the Bible that says otherwise.

The church was here when many of its members were thrown to the lions in Roman arenas, when many of its members were burned at the stake, when they were hunted in the Roman sewers, when they died lingering deaths from pestilence, when they were persecuted during the Inquisition, and now when they are being slaughtered by Muslim terrorists. It has been said that more Christians have been martyred in the 20th century than in many other centuries combined.

If I had a choice of watching my wife and kids being chewed on by lions, or being burned at the stake, or being slaughtered or sold into slavery, and on the other hand living through some extremely tough times known as the Great Tribulation, I think I'd take the latter. I might even watch quite a bit of it on CNN or Fox News.

If you were sitting in the front row of a Roman arena and you saw me running for my life from a lion, would you yell down to me, "Hey, pal, look at the good side. At least you won't have to go through the Great Tribulation!"

Yeah, thanks.

This stuff makes for good storytelling, and it sells a lot of books. But there is no biblical truth to the matter. There is a rapture of believers, but it takes place at the same time the dead are resurrected—which happens to be at the visible second coming of Christ. This is explained briefly in 1st Cor. 15:51,52 where it says:

"Behold, I tell you a mystery. We shall not all sleep, but we shall all be changed—in a moment, in the twinkling of an eye, at the last trumpet. For the trumpet will sound, and the dead will be raised incorruptible, and we shall be changed."

Those who are alive at the time of Christ's coming cannot be resurrected because they are not in the grave. So they will be raptured, or caught up. Those in the graves cannot be raptured because they are dead. So they must be resurrected. This is further explained in 1st Thess. 4:15-17.

It should be plain to see that the day of the rapture and the day of the resurrection is the same day, and both rapture and resurrection are part of the same event. Both the raptured and the resurrected will have their lowly bodies transformed that they may be conformed to His glorious body…(Phil 3:21).

This is the climactic event of the great escape.

Will you be a part of this? If not you will have to wait for the resurrection of the damned that will take place 1000 years later and stand at the great white throne judgment where you will be judged according to your works (unforgiven sin) and cast into the lake of fire (Rev. 20:5,11-15).

Good luck.

WHAT SECRET RAPTURE?

There are many well-known Bible teachers for whom I have the greatest respect. I envy their knowledge of the Word of God, especially those in Fundamentalist circles. They stand on the truth of the Bible against all comers, earnestly contending for the faith which was once for all delivered to the saints.

Yet on this one issue it is necessary to part company with them. I do this reluctantly, but as a biblicist I have no choice. In my mind and heart I desire to remain true to the Word of God as I understand it. Furthermore, I do not believe that the question of a pretribulation rapture should be a litmus test for biblical orthodoxy or Fundamentalist acceptance. In the grand scheme of things this teaching is not that important.

I once believed in the pretribulation rapture of the church because I was taught this by pastors, radio preachers, and learned laymen who articulated this particular point of view. It sounded right, and I was familiar with various Bible passages that I was told supported the belief.

But one night I attended a meeting and heard an itinerant evangelist say, "Do you know there's not one verse in the Bible that says Jesus is going to come and rapture the church out of the world before the great tribulation?"

That surprised me. Obviously this fellow didn't know what he was talking about. If there were no Scripture verses to support the belief, then what was it based upon? I decided to carefully investigate the matter.

Sure enough I found that there was not a single verse in the New Testament that literally supported the belief in a pre-trib rapture of the church. And I suddenly realized that I had always believed in a pre-trib rapture because (like the majority of those who believe this) I had been told it by others, and not because I had seen it for myself in the pages of God's word.

I began analyzing the arguments I had always heard in favor of this theory. The first thing I noticed was that the pre-trib rapture was almost an obsession with certain spokesmen for the belief. This was all they seemed to talk about. But their insistence on this point of view was not based upon a clear presentation from the Word of God. Instead the rapture was first *assumed*, and then various verses were found and made to fit the belief.

But this is interpreting the Bible backwards. It is exactly what cultists do. They propagate a teaching not found in Scripture, assume its truth, and then twist certain Bible verses to make the teaching appear legitimate. One of the most outlandish statements made by the pre-tribs is their claim that the Bible should be taken literally (and it should be, except where it is obvious from the context that it should not be) and that those who deny the pre-trib rapture are guilty of allegorizing and spiritualizing Scripture.

Yet upon examination we find that they themselves are guilty of that very thing. A classic example is found in their understanding of Rev. 4:1. This reads, "After these things I looked, and behold, a door standing open in heaven. And the first voice which I heard was like a trumpet speaking with me, saying, 'Come up here, and I will show you things which must take place after this,'"

A literal understanding of this passage teaches that the Apostle John was taken up into heaven (or had a vision to that effect) and beheld the future—period! But the pre-tribs spiritualize this verse and claim that this represents the rapture of the church.

<u>But it doesn't say that!</u> And then in the very next breath they claim they are the true biblicists who take the Bible

literally. One pre-trib TV evangelist, who emphasizes a prophetic ministry, said, "Jesus comes for the church in Revelation 4, and seven years later in Revelation 19 comes in judgment."

Yet when we read Rev. 4 we can't find Jesus coming or going anywhere. The statement is pure invention.

The pre-tribs claim that the 144,000 sealed from the twelve tribes of Israel in Rev. 7 and 14 are Jewish evangelists who will preach the gospel during the tribulation period. But there is nothing in the context of either passage showing that these 144,000 will preach anything at all. This is another false assumption.

The pre-tribs claim there will be people saved during the tribulation period (and this is true) but that they will not be members of the church because the church will have already been taken (raptured) from the earth.

<u>But where does the Bible say that?</u> Here we have another false assumption. The fact that the tribulation saints have their robes washed in the blood of the lamb (Rev. 7:14) should prove beyond any doubt that they are Christians. And if Christians are on earth getting saved during the Tribulation, then it is obvious they are members of a church that is still there. If not, this leaves the pre-tribs in the ridiculous position of believing that the church is raptured before the Tribulation, only to be replaced by another church in the Tribulation.

But why? What is the point of this fast shuffle?

"Well, don't they claim that the Tribulation saints are not part of the church because the Holy Spirit has already left the world with the true church, and that without the Holy Spirit there is no church?"

Yes, they say that. But stop and think for a moment. In the first place there is nothing in the Bible saying the Holy Spirit leaves the world just before the Tribulation. The reference to "he" in 2nd Thess. 2:7 is commonly understood to mean the ruling power (government) that restrains lawlessness, and not the Holy Spirit. To refer to the Holy

Spirit as a restrainer against sin is an overreach. Of all the ministries and offices of the Holy Spirit that are listed in Scripture, we cannot find one depicting Him as a world policeman.

One of the most damaging indictments against the pre-trib position can be found in 2nd Thess. 1:6-8. "Since it is a righteous thing with God to repay with tribulation those who trouble you, and to give you who are troubled rest with us when the Lord Jesus is revealed from heaven with His mighty angels, in flaming fire taking vengeance on those who do not know God, and on those who do not obey the gospel of our Lord Jesus Christ."
The writer is speaking to Christians, telling them that their relief is when…?
<u>When Jesus comes with His angels in flaming fire!</u> This is obviously not the picture of a secret rapture, but rather the revelation of Christ at His second coming. And we find that the church (those being addressed at the moment) will be here on earth at the time!
A reference commonly used to support the pre-trib rapture is, "For the Lord Himself will descend from heaven with a shout, with the voice of an archangel, and with the trumpet of God. And the dead in Christ will rise first. Then we who are alive and remain shall be caught up together with them in the clouds to meet the Lord in the air. And thus we shall always be with the Lord" (1st Thess. 4:16,17).
This event will most definitely happen, but there is nothing in the context saying it will happen secretly seven years before the actual Second Coming of Christ. <u>It just isn't there!</u> The fact that the events mentioned here do not match up perfectly with the events of 2nd Thess. 2:3-8 does not indicate that we are talking about two separate events, any more than the inscription on the cross of Christ mentioned in Mark 15:26, "The King Of The Jews," differing as it does with the inscription mentioned in Matt. 27:37, "This is Jesus The King Of The Jews," differing as it does with the inscription in John 19:19, "Jesus Of Nazareth The King Of

The Jews," means that we are talking about three different crosses. The full inscription on one cross obviously said, "This Is Jesus Of Nazareth The King Of The Jews."

The events depicted in 1st Thess. 4:13-17 describe the Second Coming as it relates primarily to believers; the events in 2nd Thess. 1:6-9 as it relates primarily to unbelievers; and the events in 2nd Thess. 2:3-8 as it relates primarily to the world situation at that time. All this will happen at the same time, and there is nothing in Scripture indicating a need for it to be otherwise.

To properly understand the events of the Second Coming, all passages dealing with the subject should be examined together and matched one with another in order to get the full and proper picture. This way the Bible interprets itself, and we eliminate doctrines and beliefs whose only support are stray verses taken out of context.

Another look at 1st Thess. 4:16,17 indicates that this secret rapture might not be so secret. Shouts, and the voice of an archangel, and the trumpet of God...? That sounds like a very public and cataclysmic happening. But the pre-tribs get out of this by claiming, "Oh, but only believers will hear this."

Very convenient. But again we ask, <u>Where does the Word of God say this? And where does the Bible indicate that there will be any trumpets blown before the Great Tribulation? And who shouts and blows trumpets when they are going somewhere secretly</u>?

This is another of the many unsupported assumptions upon which the pre-tribs lean for support. It is almost as bad as the wild stories about planes crashing and cars running off the road after their Christian drivers have been raptured, and the rest of mankind standing around scratching their heads wondering where everyone has gone. <u>Where is the biblical support for believing all this?</u>

Another favorite pre-trib argument is: "The church is not mentioned after the fourth chapter of Revelation, which means it is no longer on the scene. It has been caught up and is with the Lord, and no longer part of what is taking place on earth."

This is an argument from silence and is always a weak position from which to debate. Many of the scenes from Rev. 4 to Rev.19 take place in heaven, and we don't find the church mentioned there either. So where is it…?

There are saints on earth during the Tribulation, but to this the pre-tribs say, "Oh, but they are not Christians; they are saints like the Old Testament saints,"

And again we have to ask: "<u>And where does the Bible say that?</u>"

Some Pre-tribs claim that the gospel preached during the Tribulation will not be the gospel preached during the church age, but instead will be the gospel of the kingdom, equivalent to that preached by John the Baptist.

But again, "<u>Where does the Bible say that?</u>"

If every claim of the pre-tribs was countered with, "Please show me where the Bible says that?" the belief would probably be fully and finally exposed as a totally man-made doctrine not worthy of serious consideration by any thoughtful student of the Bible.

Yet its advocates can be found everywhere preaching this with a fanaticism that defies logical explanation. One noted radio Bible teacher said, "In John 14:1-3 the believers are taken out of the world to the Father's house. At the second coming of Christ the saints return to earth with Jesus to reign with Him on the earth for 1000 years. John 14:1-3 does not mention Christ coming to set up His kingdom. Therefore the rapture and the second coming must be two different events."

How's that for man-made rationalization? The same preacher goes on to say, "The catching away of the church before the time of the Tribulation is based on the definition of the church. If the term "church" applies to a specific group of people, distinct from national Israel, we can then allow for a special rapture before the Tribulation."

We can then allow…? Is this how we determine correct Bible doctrine? Why not instead point out the specific scriptural references that teach this doctrine, and never mind using the philosophy of cultists who superimpose human reasoning over their limited understanding of the Word?

Although the Tribulation will be a time of great woe on the earth, it is not the living Hell that pre-tribs would like us to believe. The worse one can do is die, and that is the act of a moment. Christians die horrible deaths every day. They have been butchered, persecuted, imprisoned, burned at the stake, and murdered for two thousand years. Some have died horrible deaths in prison camps or have been sold into slavery. The fact that they were Christians did not guarantee them immunity from this suffering. What takes place during the Tribulation can be no worse than dying from pancreatic cancer or being eaten alive by a lion in a Roman arena. Give me a choice and I think I'd take my chances running for my life and hiding out during the Tribulation.

In some quarters the pre-trib rapture theory is known as "spoiled brat" theology. Pre-tribs feel that although the church has undergone tremendous persecution and hardship in many lands throughout the past 2000 years, such times should not come to the Christians in North America. The Christians here will be whisked away from all future troubles. Big problems are evidently only for the lower class elements of the body of Christ.

This is the main danger of the pre-trib theory. It fosters a deadening effect upon Christians who should be out in their society holding up a standard of righteousness and acting like the true salt of the earth, instead of hiding in their churches waiting to be whisked away.

The Word of God is very clear on all the great doctrines of the faith. They can be found, examined, and taught with confidence. The pre-trib rapture theory cannot be found and taught with confidence. In fact it has been debated by some whether or not anyone had ever heard of it before the early 1800s.

I have no doubt that many may have been brought to a knowledge of the gospel through and best-selling Left

Behind book series. For this we can all be thankful. But I have no doubt that others have also been brought to a saving knowledge of Christ by those who did not always dot every "i" and cross every "t" properly or agree on every side issue.

But as the Apostle Paul said in Phil. 1:18, "Whether in pretense or in truth, as long as Christ is preached, in this I rejoice," and no matter which position is right concerning the events of the Second Coming, in the final analysis it really won't make that much difference.

But—if the Bible is really true, one should make every effort to understand it in its right sense, and not just according to what everyone else might be saying at the time.

THE SECOND COMING OF CHRIST

The Second Coming of Christ will signal the end of the world as we presently know it. This present age will end because the way it is now constituted it does not glorify God and does not figure into His long-range plans. And most important of all, because it is rotted through with sin!

So it will be brought to an end. But this ending will not be similar to a long walk off into the twilight while the words The End flash upon the screen.

No, it will be an ending filled with judgment and sudden destruction. The loving and gentle Jesus, the babe in Bethlehem, the One who had such compassion on the sick and lame, will return in flaming judgment to destroy and cast into Hell those who opposed Him and those who knew Him not. Read the words of the event:

"…when the Lord Jesus is revealed from heaven with His mighty angels, in flaming fire taking vengeance on those who do not know God, and on those who do not obey the gospel of our Lord Jesus Christ. These shall be punished with everlasting destruction from the presence of the Lord and from the glory of His power" (2nd Thess. 1:7-9).

Those who do not know God…? Well, there are plenty of them. Those who do not obey the gospel of Jesus Christ…? There are plenty of them. And they will evidently be in very big trouble. In light of what we have discovered so far, these two groups will make up the majority of the human race at that time. The Second Coming of Christ, then, is not something the world should be eagerly awaiting.

Notice the words in vs. 8, "taking vengeance." That is an attitude and frame of mind that we do not ordinarily associate with God. A Bible dictionary defines vengeance as "punishment in retaliation for an injury or offense; repayment for a wrong suffered," and Webster's Dictionary is almost word for word the same.

Yet did not God say, "You shall not take vengeance, nor bear any grudge against the children of your people, but you shall love your neighbor as yourself...?" (Lev. 19:18).

He did. Because vengeance is not for man. The Apostle Paul wrote, "Beloved, do not avenge yourselves, but rather give place to wrath; for it is written 'Vengeance is mine. I will repay' says the Lord" (Rom. 12:19).

It is God who takes vengeance. Read what He said against the Philistines: "Thus says the Lord God. Because the Philistines dealt vengefully and took vengeance with a spiteful heart, to destroy because of an old hatred...I will stretch out My hand against the Philistines...I will execute great vengeance on them with furious rebukes; and they shall know that I am the Lord, when I lay my vengeance upon them" (Ez. 25:15-17).

And so shall Jesus Christ take vengeance upon this rebellious world when He comes in flaming fire with His angels.

The details of how all this will happen are scattered from Matthew to Revelation. Some of the most graphic descriptions of the event are found in Matthew 24 and 25. Jesus is speaking here and lays out for His listeners the sequence of events that will take place when He comes again, what will happen immediately afterwards, and why it is necessary to watch and be ready for His coming.

First of all, there will be many religious phonies arriving on the scene as we near the end. He says there will be wars and rumors of war, but not to worry about them because the end is not yet. He says nation will rise against nation, and there will be famines and earthquakes...and that this is just the beginning of our sorrows. He says His followers will be hunted down and killed. False prophets will rise up, lawlessness will increase, and people will be concerned only about themselves.

After all hell breaks loose for a time "Then the sign of the Son of Man will appear in heaven, and then all the tribes of the earth will mourn (note, they will not be cheering or rejoicing over this great event), and they will see the Son of Man coming on the clouds of heaven with power and great glory. And He will send His angels with a great sound of a trumpet, and they will gather together His elect from the four winds, from one end of heaven to the other" (Matt. 24:30,31).

This time is known as The Day Of The Lord. There are a number of books in the New Testament that describe events at the end time, some very briefly, and others only two or three verses. But they must be considered pieces of the whole.

As we have just read, Matthew 24 has quite a bit to say on the subject. But 2nd Thess. 2:3 adds some important information. Here we learn that That Day will not come until there is first a falling away from the faith, and the man of sin is revealed—he being the antichrist described in vs. 4. When this individual is running things in his part of the world, then, when no one suspects it, Jesus Christ will return, destroy this satanically powered individual, and set in motion events that will bring about the end of this present age.

The end will be judgment of this world system, and also judgment upon most of mankind.

The dead will also be raised at the Second Coming, and this we have mentioned in 1st Cor. 15. This chapter explains the intricacies of the resurrection, the nature of the resurrection body, and the interesting fact that Christians who are living on earth on that day will never physically die. They will be changed in the wink of an eye and given their resurrection bodies in which they will live for eternity.

If we were to broadcast over network news tonight that next Tuesday at 1:30 in the afternoon Jesus Christ will come to this earth for the second time, and this time as judge and ruler, millions of people would go out of their minds. The stock market would probably crash, some people would shoot themselves, some would be filling churches around the clock, and others—believe it or not—would be getting their guns and artillery ready to fight Him off.

You don't think so? Then read Psalm 2. From the Garden of Eden all the way to the end of this age, man does not want God telling him what to do. He wants to be his own god, the captain of his own ship. "Let us break their bonds in pieces and cast away their cords from us" (vs. 3) is their cry.

But God laughs at this (vs. 4) and orders His son (vs. 9) to smash them to pieces. But He suggests first that they smarten up to avoid this (vs. 10-12).

The God of the Bible, contrary to what liberal clergy and muddleheaded media personnel might think, is not the soft touch of their imaginations. Nor is He controlled or impressed by their pronouncements, views, ideas or philosophy, societal or spiritual. He has revealed Himself in the Bible and nowhere else. The God you find in the Bible is the one you have to deal with, like it or not!

In the Bible God has given rules, restrictions, laws, and a lifestyle to which He expects you to conform. He has also taught doctrines He expects you to believe. Most of these doctrines concern Jesus Christ, whom He sent to ransom you from the penalty of your sins. "Just as the Son of Man did not come to be served, but to serve, and give His life a ransom for many" (Matt. 20:28).

The doctrines concerning Christ are the doctrines that teach the sinner how to save his soul. Without a knowledge of these doctrines the individual sinner walks in darkness, spiritually blind, with no hope, and no future—except that of eternal damnation.

"Hold on, hold on, there must be some other way—"

No, there is no other way. The Bible says, "For there is one God, and one mediator between God and men, the man

Christ Jesus" (1 Tim. 2:5). That's it. Allah, Buddha, Vishnu, and anyone else you may want to throw in will do you no good. In fact they will probably do you more harm than good, as their beliefs will blind you to the truth. This, of course, is assuming that the Bible is really true, and that Jesus knew exactly what he was talking about.

"Well if you pray and tell God that you're sorry for your sins just before you die, He will forgive you and everything will be OK, no matter who you are."

That sounds good except for one thing: Jesus never said that, nor does Christian doctrine even throw a hint in that direction.

When judgment day comes you will not be able to talk your way out of anything. God does not automatically listen to everyone's prayer. "One who turns away his ear from hearing the law, even his prayer is an abomination" (Prov. 28:9). So don't think you're going to get an automatic audience with God just because you're yelling in His direction from your deathbed. Listen to what God said about His own chosen ones in the book of Jeremiah when they went bad:

"Behold I will surely bring calamity on them which they will not be able to escape; and though they cry out to Me, I will not listen to them" (Jer. 11:11).

And as far as anyone else putting in a good word for you, forget it!

"Then the Lord said to me, 'Even if Moses and Samuel stood before Me, My mind would not be favorable toward this people. Cast them out of My sight...'" (Jer. 15:1).

If you have not been saved, then at the end of your life you will stand all alone, cut off from a God who wants nothing to do with you.

You can see that this last minute stuff is no guarantee of anything. If you live like a child of Hell all your life, with no knowledge or understanding of the simple gospel of Christ you will not be disposed to true repentance on judgment day. Without that repentance God will not listen to you. (In fact judgment day will probably be one day too late to repent anyway.)

"Because you disdained all My counsel, and would have none of My rebuke, I will also laugh at your calamity; I will mock when your terror comes. When your terror comes like a storm, and your destruction comes like a whirlwind. When distress and anguish come upon you.

"Then they will call on Me but I will not answer; They will seek Me diligently, but they will not find Me. Because they hated knowledge and did not choose the fear of the Lord" (Prov.1:25-29).

If the Bible is really true, you could very easily find yourself in this position.

And then even worse....

THE FLY IN THE OINTMENT

If the Bible is really true, then the preaching of the gospel is the most important of all professions. The man in the pulpit is literally more important than any king or president. Kings and presidents rule and deal with the here and now. The preacher deals with issues of eternity. What he says can affect you more profoundly than anything said by other men.

Unfortunately all preachers do not match up with their responsibilities. We are speaking here mainly of Protestant preachers, as Roman Catholic and Orthodox priests are not preachers in the true sense of the word, their function being more ceremonial. The true preacher is one who stands in a pulpit, opens a Bible, and preaches from a text.

The problem is in what many of them actually preach. Some take a subject of possible religious significance, draw upon their knowledge and background, quote a Bible verse or two, and from all this attempt to make their case.

On the surface this might make for an interesting thirty-minute talk, especially if it's spiced with one or two humorous comments. Also, the preacher has the chance to illustrate just how learned he is, how fluent he can be, the fact that he is well-read, and how important he is as a fount of wisdom for his congregation.

Hooray for the preacher!

Unfortunately this approach does not prove that this man is a Bible preacher. And a preacher who is not a solid Bible preacher is a preacher who is short-changing his congregation.

The simplest explanation of a true Bible preacher can be found in Nehemiah 8:8 where it is written, "So they read distinctly from the book, in the Law of God, and they gave the sense, and helped them to understand the reading."

The man who does this is a Bible preacher because he (1) presents the Word of God, (2) gives the right sense (or angle) of the text, and (3) then helps his listeners to fully understand what was written. Added to this he convinces, rebukes and exhorts his listeners (2nd Tim. 4:2), in the context of warning and teaching them (Col. 1:28).

You do not need a seminary education to understand this. It's all written plainly in your Bible. You just have to read it.

A church service is supposed to be for the benefit of those sitting in the pews. These people get out of bed on one of their possible two days off a week, get their families cleaned up, drive to church, meet a lot of other nice people, and then are sometimes forced to sit and listen to a lecture from a clergyman who has apparently forgotten why he wanted to be a preacher in the first place.

People should not attend church and be forced to listen to lectures. And lectures are what they many times hear. If you attend church you should be given the privilege of hearing the Word of God explained and expounded. You should hear questions of eternal significance discussed and debated; you should hear an oral address on truth contained in the Scriptures that is elaborately treated with a view to persuasion.

The last thing you need is a lecture about some incident, person, or problem that deviates from the Word of God, or a simplistic explanation of a familiar truth garnished with an "interesting twist" that is used to illustrate the preacher's perceptiveness. Nor do you need a sermon given only to make some "generic" religious or ethical point. When it is mentioned at the close of a service that next week professor so-and-so from some seminary or college will be here speaking on "The Church In Today's World" (or some other amorphous subject), that is when you should make immediate plans to stay home and mow the lawn. This stuff you do not need! Material of this nature should be fed to young students in seminary classrooms, and not to mature believers in the faith.

The essence of preaching can be found in a statement made by the Apostle Paul when he said, concerning Christ, "Him we preach, warning every man and teaching every man in all wisdom, that we may present every man perfect in Christ Jesus" (Col. 1:28).

There are two fundamental aspects of real biblical preaching and they consist of *warning* and *teaching* that is based strictly on the Word of God and not on the latest social or ecclesiastical trends.

What does warning and teaching do? Evidently, if done right, it works toward "presenting every man perfect in Christ Jesus."

This seems like a simple enough directive. Yet in our present church climate it is becoming more of a rarity. A growing number of Bible believing Christians no longer attend church regularly because of the spiritual pabulum constantly spewed from the pulpit. They long for the solid meat of the Word, but are instead presented with a steady diet of milk…or with sermons that say essentially nothing, delivered by men whose doctrinal thinking and subsequent teachings are simply repetitions of what they heard in the classroom, instead of what has been revealed to their hearts by the careful and personal study of the Word of God.

The majority of sermons should fit into one of two categories. First, you preach to convert. Second, you preach to build up in holiness and doctrinal purity those who are converted. A ministry based on these two simple fundamentals will be a fruitful ministry that will lead to a growing church. People will be excited because they are learning, and learning is still fun even if dealing with matters of extreme gravity. All other positive aspects of a ministry should be classified as secondary, and that includes providing for the material needs of others, complaining about abortion, walking for hunger, and things of that nature. It is good to be concerned about the physical well-being of others, but it should not be the primary focus of ministry. As one Fundamentalist preacher said, "Preaching is to the church what food is to a restaurant. It's the reason you go there."

Many people mistakenly think that a church exists only to take care of the needs of others. Example:

One day a woman carrying a small rabbit walked into a large downtown Boston church. She said, "Could you take care of this rabbit? No one wants him."

The sexton said, "Lady, this isn't a zoo. We don't take care of rabbits here."

The woman, a bit upset at this answer, said, "Well, this is a church, isn't it?"

At other times people have come into this same church with stories of how they were robbed or lost their money and need train fare back home. When told that the church does not pass out money to everyone who shows up at the front door, the response a number of times has been, "Well what kind of a church is this? Aren't you supposed to care about people?"

These examples might be a bit extreme, but they typify the thinking of millions who have been led to believe that a local church is a mini-welfare agency. Churches are supposed to help people, they claim. That's what they're for. Don't they preach from their pulpits that people should do more to help others? Didn't Jesus say that we should love everybody? (I don't think so.)

Compassion is in. And it should be "in" in the church of Jesus Christ.

But there's a bit more to the function of a church than that. The true church exists to give people a message—not a handout.

Many churches that are doctrinally sound suffer because the man in the pulpit is a disaster as a public speaker. If you are not naturally a good public speaker, then you have no business in the pulpit of a church in the first place, because a preacher—before anything—is first a public speaker. What good is it for a man to have three degrees if what he says does not come across clear and interesting and intelligible?

Regardless of what you may think of his political beliefs, Sen. Ted Kennedy, in his prime, was one of the best public speakers you could hear. His voice was full, clear, and he knew how to project. Even if you disagreed with everything he said, it was interesting listening to him.

Yet in many churches we have men in the pulpit who drone on in a conversational manner, whose thoughts are rambling and disorganized, and whose dull monotone does a better job on the congregation than a barrel full of sleeping pills. But they have all kinds of fancy degrees. Well good for them. But tough on us.

Shouldn't our concern be more for the guy in the pew who is worrying about whether or not his kid will turn into a solid Christian or a bum, or if his wife is going to survive her cancer, or if his brother is going to Hell, or if he's doing the right thing by going into business with a Muslim? These are cutting edge issues with many people and they expect to hear something hard and clear and biblical that will give them some needed information and direction.

But this character in the pulpit with his lectures about the latest Walk For Hunger, or Should We Allow Gays In The Ministry (if he doesn't already know the answer to that he shouldn't be in the ministry himself), or What Direction Should The Church Take In The Next Century, is doing him no good. The rubber is not hitting the road here.

Degrees do not make a preacher. A heartfelt concern for the lost is what makes a preacher. I have personally seen churches almost ruined because the goal of the pulpit committee was to find the most brilliantly educated man they could afford. How many degrees does he have? Where did he graduate? Where did he get his doctorate?

Whereas the concern should have been: How many converts did he have at his last church? Is he good at personal evangelism? How much time does he spend in prayer and personal Bible study?

One church I know of got its educated man of whom they were very proud. But over the next few years no one got converted, people did not bring their friends to church to hear this man (primarily because he never said anything they thought their friends would find interesting or important), and attendance began to dwindle. The church finally became like so many others, a half-empty shell that ended up existing solely for its own sake.

But no one denied that the minister is a very educated man.

The Bible says, "This is a faithful saying and worthy of all acceptance, that Christ Jesus came into the world to save sinners…" (1st Tim.1:15). If your ministry is not based on that simple truth then you'd be better off selling insurance or maybe teaching school. Preaching the need to be saved, and how Jesus saves sinners, is the bedrock of gospel preaching.

The Bible also says, "Preach the word! Be ready in season and out of season. Convince, rebuke, exhort, with all long-suffering and teaching" (2nd Tim.4:2). Those three words, convince, rebuke, exhort, is where it's at! This is preaching. And it's all done within the context of the last word, *teaching*.

Some might remember the old gangster movies of the 1940s when the policeman would grab the tough guy (many times James Cagney) and read him the riot act, trying to straighten him out. And the tough guy would snarl back, "Don't waste your time preaching to me, copper!"

And that's exactly what the policeman was doing. He was preaching. He would attempt to *convince* the tough guy to straighten out, he would *rebuke* him for breaking the law, and he would *exhort* him to follow the straight and narrow path.

In the same sense this is what a preacher should be doing when addressing sinners. The sinner is not going to get anything from a philosophical lecture on Discovering Your Leadership Qualities, or an intellectual sermon on The

Christian Response To Living In A Consumer Oriented Society. You have to come down to where people live.

(Maybe we need more cops in our pulpits.)

If the Bible is really true, and its message the most important message one can hear, then that message should be communicated in the most competent manner possible by those who possess the right physical, mental, and spiritual equipment. Anything less could do more damage than good by boring people to the point where they finally drop out of church altogether.

Many times, whether we like it or not, it is necessary to fire a pastor (preacher) for incompetence. This is easier said than done, as there are always some in every church who mistakenly feel they must always support the pastor regardless of the situation.

The folly of this position was made evident by the almost total disintegration of an independent Baptist church in a town approximately 18 miles northwest of Boston. This church had an average Sunday attendance of roughly 150 worshippers. The present pastor had been called to fill the pulpit after a minor church split had caused the previous pastor to leave.

Things went along smoothly for about seven or eight months. But then it slowly became evident to many in the congregation that this man wasn't a very good preacher after all, and that his sermons had no depth. This congregation was used to solid Bible preaching.

Statements like, "This man's not saying anything—He never gets into any doctrine—He's a nice guy, but he can't preach" were heard around the church with increasing frequency.

The deacons mentioned these concerns to the pastor, but the pastor waved them off and seemed offended that anyone could think like this. He defended his ministry.

Opposition from the more spiritually mature members of the congregation became more vocal. But the deacons were afraid to make this public for fear of again dividing the church. So they kept silent, but did fault the pastor in the privacy of board meetings.

The discontent grew. People were no longer inviting their friends to church. One family decided to leave. The pastor said there were some he would never be able to please, and that he was not a theologian anyway, but a pastor, and a pastor was what the church needed. But growing numbers in the church insisted that what the church really needed was a strong Bible teaching ministry, claiming this kind of ministry would strengthen the church and attract new members.

Three deacons finally quit the church and never came back. The pastor said the church would carry on without them. New deacons were appointed who supported the pastor.

But many in the congregation still complained, claiming that if the pastor stayed on the church would go nowhere. As the weeks went by more people began leaving. But many of those on the official board of the church still supported the pastor's ministry, claiming that he was God's anointed for the church and that if God called him to serve here he should be supported by the people.

Church attendance and income were now dangerously low. Some suggested that the pastor was hanging on only for the paycheck, and that it was now obvious he had no real concern for the church or its spiritual welfare. Why didn't he leave?

Factions developed. Grumbling continued in the parking lot, the rest rooms, and over the telephone. The pastor tried to keep a lid on the discontent. The official board continued to support the pastor, insisting he was a fine man and that it was a shame he had to put up with all the bickering and dissension. There were obviously groups of troublemakers in the congregation.

Bills began to mount and the church fell deeper into debt. The pastor ignored this and said the church was experiencing a new beginning. He urged the congregation to invite friends and others to church. But no friends came, and people continued to leave.

Finally the three men left on the official board informed the pastor they would have no money to pay him past the coming week. The pastor finally resigned, blaming others for the church's problems.

Right now this church is struggling to keep its doors open. Its witness is gone and its reputation is in tatters. Most of those who left said they would not go back under any circumstances.

This is a tragedy, but it could have been avoided if the leadership of the church had placed the importance of the message ahead of the importance of the messenger. If a pastor does not preach the Word of God effectively then he should be replaced, even if he is a fine old fellow in other aspects of ministry. If you can bench or trade a quarterback or shortstop because they aren't producing, then why should a church be forced to put up with a pastor who is not producing? And the idea that "I feel that God has called me here to serve so I'm staying" should be ignored or challenged with "Well we feel that God has called us together to tell you that you should leave, so please turn in your resignation."

One claim is just as good as the other.

It is no secret that there is a lack of good Bible teachers in America's pulpits. Many small churches, recognizing this, have dismissed their pastors and gone over to a lay ministry, hiring laymen from the congregation (or area) to teach the Bible and get back to the basics of getting sinners converted.

This is not to make light of a seminary education, but too many of these young kids, with little or no real life experience, know nothing except what they have heard in school and end up sounding like windup dolls from whose back you expect to see a big slow-turning silver key. Nor do they understand that a good preacher preaches from "the overflow," and not just his notes.

The lay preachers usually eliminate the empty sermons on family living, e.g., *How To Beat Depression, Make Your Marriage Last Forever, Raising Your Teenager,* sermons that turn church into "adult story hour," and sermons in which the church is always the main subject, as if somehow messages about the organization were more important than messages about sin, salvation, and the Savior. *The Mission Of The Church In The New Millennium* is a classic example of what we don't need (and what a lay preacher probably couldn't preach anyway. But who cares…?).

If the Bible is really true its main message should not be placed on the back burner. Too much of the evangelical church has been polluted to the point where ministries spend more time teaching people how to solve the problems of daily life than they do teaching them how to obtain the right kind of afterlife. Could you imagine reading the book of Acts and hearing the Apostle Paul, when coming into a city like Ephesus or Corinth, address the people with sermons titled, *How to Manage Your Money,* or *Have You Felt Like Giving Up Lately?* or *Making Your Life Make Sense,* or *Your Work Matters To God,* or any of the other slap-happy issues that have unfortunately replaced solid biblical teaching?

The early church never would have gotten off the ground! The message of the book of Acts is best put by Peter's statement, "Repent therefore and be converted, that your sins may be blotted out…" (Acts 3:19), because if you are not converted and your sins are not blotted out—you will perish forever in Hell (even if you do know How To Manage Your Money).

That is a message worthy of attention. Everything else is secondary. Assuming, or course, that the Bible is true as written.

YOU <u>CAN</u> ARGUE RELIGION

Have you ever heard someone say, "There are two things you can't argue about, religion and politics?"

You probably have, as it's a very popular position to take whenever these subjects come up for discussion. The one making the statement will speak with an artificial air of wisdom that he expects will not be challenged, and fully expects his comments to close down all further debate.

But on close examination we usually find that the speaker is someone who knows absolutely nothing about either subject. You cannot argue about these subjects because he will be left out of the argument, and this he does not want. So he levels the playing field by informing everyone it would be useless to further discuss these issues.

But his argument has no weight. You can argue both religion and politics. Just ask those involved in either field. People heavily involved in politics can talk and argue about the subject all night. The same holds true for those involved in religion. They can debate the value and correctness of their theological positions for hours with both friend and foe, and if they know how to do this correctly, end the debate with a smile.

This is especially true for those who make a habit of reading and studying the Bible. The Bible itself tells us to "...contend earnestly for the faith which was once for all delivered to the saints" (Jude 1:3b).

Again, the dictionary. Contend: "to struggle in opposition; to dispute earnestly." Or in other words, to put up a darn good argument for what you believe!

There is nothing wrong with this. In fact it is essential for the propagation of the faith. If a particular belief cannot hold its own in the marketplace of ideas it should be cast aside. Why would anyone want to support or follow a losing argument?

But Christianity does not lose in open debate. It can hold its own, and does so very effectively when it takes the offensive. It is understood that you cannot argue a person into the kingdom of God by the force of argument alone. Yet God does use the limits of our intelligence and talents to carry out the divine program, even the limits of our ability to argue and press home our points.

How does He do that? Let us look at the many examples recorded in the book of Acts. First of all, notice that the Apostle Paul never hesitated to walk right into the midst of the ideological opposition. In Acts 13:14 we find him arriving in Antioch and heading straight for the synagogue. When a ruler of the synagogue asked if anyone would like to speak, Paul stood up and preached a short sermon that in some parts could be considered antagonistic. But he did not hesitate to speak because the circumstances might not have been favorable, nor did he fear walking into the camp of the enemy. In one sense he almost went looking for trouble. But the result was the preaching of the Word of God to those in need. If he was a troublemaker it was to the glory of God.

Acts 16:37 relates how, after being beaten unjustly by the authorities, Paul, in righteous indignation, humbled those same authorities by forcing them to release him instead of sending him away quietly to hide their wrongdoing.

The Apostle Paul did not just preach the Word and then pull out of the situation. He reasoned with his theological opponents.

But many Christians look upon reasoning with suspicion because they assume that man is trying to force what only God can accomplish. However this is an unfair analysis. Paul reasoned, argued, and disputed with his opponents at every turn. He knew that God was the final arbiter of what would happen, but this was never used as an excuse to leave the field of intellectual battle.

Acts 18:4 says that Paul "reasoned in the synagogue" and "persuaded both Jews and Greeks." That sounds like the very ultimate in human effort. But what's wrong with the ultimate in human effort when it comes to fighting for men's souls? When God uses a person to spread His word He uses that person in his total capacity. If a person is skilled and talented in debate then those abilities will be employed. If this were not true then how can we account for the varying degrees of success among disciples of the Lord even though they are all preaching the same truth?

Again in Acts 19:8 Paul is entering boldly into the synagogue reasoning with and persuading the Jews. If a man did that today he would be considered an agitator and troublemaker (and most likely a bigot or some kind of racist, guilty of saying things that some might find offensive. This is the new American crime, saying something that *offends* someone, as if there were some new constitutional right not to be offended--which there is not!)

In this country at the present time many do not dare speak out publicly against what they considers wrong religious belief because they could be accused of hate speech. In 2003 America nothing is wrong because there are no absolutes. Everything is good, everyone has rights. The bigotry of saying, "I think that point of view is wrong" cannot be tolerated. It is politically incorrect.

But in the real world there are beliefs that are good, and there are beliefs that are bad and wrong. Heaven help the one who does not know the difference, and shame on the Christian who does not publicly point this out.

In Acts 21:27-40 we can see the trouble Paul got into because of his refusal to keep quiet about his faith. He was stormed by mobs, threatened with death, and bound with chains. He threw whole cities into confusion.

How did he do it? Simply by rising up publicly and stating what he believed and not worrying about who might be offended. If he inadvertently had to make someone else's beliefs look foolish that did not stop him. The result of this activity was God's blessing upon his ministry.

The evangelical church today is too gutless to follow the same program of witness and evangelism. They are too busy with interfaith services and "better understanding each other" and 'building upon what we have in common."

But to what purpose? Whose soul will be turned from Hell to Heaven because these ministers better understand each other's beliefs? Who will be brought under conviction of his need of Christ at an interfaith service where the way of salvation cannot be mentioned because it might be considered divisive?

When the Word of God is preached the way it is supposed to be preached it becomes an extremely divisive message. There will always be a division between those who believe and those who do not believe, just as there is a division between those who are alive and those who are dead.

The best example of this difference can be found in Eph. 2:1-3 where the writer says, "And you He made alive who were dead in trespasses and sins."

Unless you are converted to Christ you are dead! It cannot be more clear-cut. But the average person does not consider himself spiritually dead; but then, with no spiritual understanding, what does he know anyway? If one is not familiar with the Bible's teaching there is no way he can understand his present danger. He is like a lamb being led to the slaughter. He walks according to the "course of this world"; meaning, he allows the world system to set his standards and beliefs. If his world is impressed with something, then he is impressed with it. If his society pans something, then he pans it. If the opinion makers of his day tell him to listen to the ideas and spiritual beliefs of some spiritually stupid rock star, then he listens to the ideas and beliefs of the spiritually stupid rock star. And why shouldn't he? Everyone else is listening, aren't they…?

What he does not realize is "the prince of the power of the air" is running this whole show from behind the scenes.

Satan works in ways he never sees and little understands. It is this very Devil who works in the lives of those who do not belong to Christ. They are known as "the sons of disobedience" (vs. 2).

This is an extremely dangerous situation in which to live. You are being set up to get hit bad. The wrath of God is hanging over your head like the sword of Damocles, and there is no way out of this mess except through conversion to Christ. Jesus said, speaking of Himself, "He who believes in Him (Christ) is not condemned; but he who does not believe is condemned already…" (John 3:18). You may be walking around quite happy and healthy at the moment, but up above you is a big fist following everywhere you go, and the minute you die it is going to slam down on you like the hammer of God to finish you off for eternity.

One does not have to wait until judgment day to find out whether or not he made it. You are being told right now that you haven't made it. You are sitting on death row waiting for the sentence to be carried out. You are like Abimelech in Gen. 20:3 who was about to start messing with Abraham's wife, and God said to him, "You're a dead man because of the woman whom you have taken, for she is a man's wife."

That's tough talk. God is telling Abimelech he's already as good as dead because of what he intends with Abraham's wife. In like manner you can consider yourself as good as dead if you are not now united with Christ through faith in His shed blood for your sins.

You may not like this, but that's the way it is. Continue in your stubbornness and you will die. But if you break and repent of your sins and are converted to Christ you will then live—assuming, of course, that the Bible is really true.

"Yeah, well if it says that then I doubt if it is true."

Okay, fine. No one is bending your arm. You are free to think what you like.

"You know, all those other religions have their Bibles and holy books and they consider them the truth."

Yeah, but they're wrong.

"How do you know?"
Check them out

Other religions have no savior from sin, no perfect plan of salvation, no prophetic element, no plan for the ages, nothing that brings one into a personal relationship with God, no assurance of redemption, etc. It's so bad that Muslim terrorists, for example, are actually taught that they will go to Paradise if they get killed while in the process of killing Jews or other innocent people. This is religiously sponsored, cold-blooded murder. Are we going to equate that with the message of the Christian gospel?

Brief as it might be, the above has been a religious argument. It can be expanded, and I'm sure improved, and used in the propagation of the faith. It is similar in some ways to those arguments used in the book of Acts. To claim that this is not a legitimate method for spreading the gospel exhibits a massive ignorance of the Bible. You can—and if you believe it, you should—argue religion.
So much could depend upon it.

REAL CHRISTIANITY

We live in an age dominated by the big scam, the con game, the swindle, and what one TV network refers to as The Fleecing of America.

Everyone seems to be ripping off everyone else. You don't know whom to trust or what to believe. Breathe on someone the wrong way and you're liable to be charged with sexual harassment; offend someone and you might get hit with a lawsuit. Invest some money in stocks and your broker steals it. It's getting so bad you expect to someday pick up the morning paper and read that George Washington was really a gangster, that the Pope heads the Mafia, and that evangelist Billy Graham, on the side, ran a nationwide money laundering organization for a terrorist network, and that Mother Teresa owned a string of brothels.

It is possible to get ripped off religiously. But we are not talking here about money. Money is petty stuff when compared to a person's soul. I am talking about fakers and con men who sound good and pious for the sole purpose of exploiting others and in the process endangering their souls.

If you want to be an on-the-ball Christian in today's world you have to know what's going on. You can't go along with something just because it has the name Jesus Christ attached to it.

Consider the Jewish exorcists in Acts 19:13 who tried using the name of Jesus to further their business. They had no real knowledge or understanding of Christian belief. They had no experience of salvation. But they knew there was something special about this Jesus and they wanted in on the action. They could smell money.

If you were in the neighborhood at the time would these people have impressed you because they were throwing around the name of Jesus? Are you impressed now when you read in the papers or see on TV certain individuals who quote a Bible verse to strengthen their political, social or religious argument?

Don't be. Religion can be greatly misused by those who are only interested in pushing their point of view for material gain.

The Jewish exorcists did not get very far in their attempt to misuse the name of Jesus. In fact they were beaten so bad they lost most of their clothes in the fight. They were obviously out of their league and paid the price for trying to fake their way into the big time.

There are many so-called Christians who will some day pay a big price for trying to fake their way through the Christian life. You can always fake out the guy in the next pew, or your next-door neighbor, and maybe a close friend. But you can't fake out God. In fact you can't even fake out the Devil, as our scene illustrates. The evil spirit went after these sons of a Jewish priest with no regard for the fact that they were connected to a respected religious family.

The powers of darkness could also go after you if you are not protected by the indwelling Holy Spirit. Without a personal relationship with Jesus Christ your religion is worth no more to you than it was to the seven sons of Sceva. Playing at religion and playing at church can be just as worthless (and dangerous) as having no religion at all.

It's the personal connection that makes the difference. It's all in who you know. That may not sound very fair as far as the world is concerned. Every time we hear the phrase, "It's not what you know, but who you know," it reeks of unfairness and maybe even discrimination. "I could have made the team but so-and-so's father knows the coach so he got picked instead." Or, "I should have gotten the job, but the supervisor is a good friend of Susan's mother, so Susan got the job instead of me," are familiar complaints.

So we rave and rant about the unfairness of a world that bases everything upon knowing the right people and having the right connections. And our complaint is valid. This is unfair.

But not when it comes to Christianity. If you are a Christian "it's not what you know but who you know" is legitimate. Personal relationship is what it's all about. If you are saved and heading for Heaven when you die it will be because you have the right connections, because you know the right person. It will not be because of anything you did, or how important you are in this world, or if you led a good moral life, or if Time Magazine just voted you Saint of the Year.

"What kind of rip-off is this? That's the most unfair thing I ever heard of. Under that system you could be the biggest bum in town and make out just because you know the right people."

That's right. The thief on the cross was probably the biggest bum in town at that time and he made out. And unfair...? Not at all. The invitation is open to everyone and there is no price tag attached. It couldn't be more fair. "Incline your ear and come to Me. Hear and your soul shall live..." (Is. 55:3).

But there will always be those who want to do things their way, and they are asking for trouble! The people in Acts 19:13 tried their hand at playing religion and it didn't work out. Don't be like them. Get "connected" and establish a right relationship with God by believing on and receiving Jesus Christ as your personal savior.

One thing you must not do is get off track. Real Christianity has to do with saving souls. It has very little (if anything) to do with learning how to experience a happy and successful life here on earth, or of beating depression, or getting along with your in-laws, or building self-esteem in your children, or improving your marriage, or whatever....

Real Christianity is concerned first and foremost with saving sinners from the wrath of God, and not with first introducing them to all the fringe benefits of the faith. The Apostle Paul says we are to wait for God's son "whom He raised from the dead, even Jesus who delivers us from the wrath to come" (1st Thess. 1:10).

Can you draw a bead on that? Can you sweep out of the way all the fakery and folderol that many Christian preachers and publishing houses serve up to make sure you will be the most well-adjusted sap who ever walked into Hell?

"Hey, what are you trying to do, scare people into becoming Christians with all this wrath stuff?"

If that's what it takes—yes! Because *wrath* is what's coming. Five minutes after you die might not be the beginning of one big picnic. It might instead be the beginning of one long nightmare...even if you did have a wonderful marriage, and maintained your health, and were very successful on your job, and had lots of self-esteem, and had even straightened out your financial problems.

Jesus Christ came to save sinners. He did not come to show you how to beat everyday problems, or conquer your fears, or lose weight, or raise your kids, or get along better with your spouse, or find peace, or improve your finances, or show you how to set goals, or how to get a handle on your career, or...please, enough of this!

Jesus said very plainly that He had come to "give His life a ransom for many" (cf. Matt. 20:28). Understanding and acting upon this is what Real Christianity is all about. Real Christianity does not place its main focus on family values entertainment, or pro-life activities, or getting rid of your hang-ups. We have no business replacing a life of self-denial with a life of self-realization. This is not the message of the cross.

One of the main purveyors of this kind of thinking is Christian psychologist, Dr. James Dobson. Dobson has a very successful ministry propagating the fringe benefits of the faith, and what he teaches is good and helpful to many. But the early church did not turn the world upside down with this kind of program—and it won't do it now!

But from a financial point of view this program is very successful and it has made Dobson a power in evangelical circles. This, of course, has then attracted our present day sons of Sceva. They can smell the money this approach generates and they adjust their ministries accordingly. Now we have a flood of evangelical books pushing family values, happy teenagers, lasting marriages, self-awareness, how to make stress work for you, and whatnot, all making big bucks.

Who is paying the big bucks? Both Christians and others who are concerned mainly with themselves. But is all this stuff really Christian literature? And are all these sons of Sceva legitimate to begin with? It doesn't take much to give others advice on how to live. Any agnostic can browse through the Psalms and book of Proverbs, find something that sounds good and makes sense, and then make his case. It's not that hard. And you don't even have to believe what you are writing as long as you're convinced that others will believe it. Satan was the first con man to quote Scripture, and he obviously will not be the last.

If the Bible is really true you are better off sticking with its main message and leaving the "feminized, inspirational comfort material" in the background. (Unless you are talking with your grandmother.) It's an easy way to stay on the straight and narrow path and avoid unnecessary confusion and distraction.

JUDGMENT DAY

Hollywood has yet to create a disaster movie that will equal or even come close to what awaits this world at the time of Christ's return.

And He will return!

Of this we can be sure.

Jesus promised many times in the gospel accounts that He would come back. "Then the sign of the Son of Man will appear in heaven, and then all the tribes of the earth will mourn (again, there will be mourning and not cheering), and they will see the Son of Man coming on the clouds of heaven with power and great glory" (Matt. 24:30).

Angels said that He would return. "This same Jesus who was taken up from you into heaven, will so come in like manner as you saw Him go into heaven" (Acts 1:11).

New Testament writers mentioned the event many times. "For you yourselves know perfectly that the day of the Lord so comes as a thief in the night. For when they say 'Peace and safety' then sudden destruction comes upon them, as labor pains upon a pregnant woman. And they shall not escape" (1st Thess. 5:2,3).

If the Bible is really true, this world system has a date with disaster. Consider the way the Apostle Peter describes it: "…the heavens will pass away with a great noise, and the elements will melt with fervent heat; both the earth and the works that are in it will be burned up" (2nd Peter 3:10).

Let's see Hollywood special effects top that.

But what kind of God would do this? What kind of God thinks so little of this present world system and the people in it that He is going to come back and literally wreck the place?

The answer is, the only God there is, and He is described in the only book that speaks about Him, the Bible.

"Yeah, well I don't believe in a God like that. That's not the God I hear about when I go to church."

Then you had better change churches—and fast! Unless you're just looking for a place to snooze for an hour or so every Sunday morning.

"But haven't you ever heard of Christian compassion? Don't you know that Jesus is a very compassionate person? It's in the Bible you're always quoting."

Yes, Jesus is compassionate—up to a point. But when you go past that point, when one flatly refuses the grace of God and free gift of eternal life through Christ, then you must deal with a God who is a consuming fire (Heb. 12:29).

"That's your opinion."

No it's not. It's exactly what the Bible says.

"You can't take that stuff literally. That's figurative writing."

The Bible does contain figurative writing. But the fact that the wicked are going to get slammed into Hell and tormented night and day forever is made plain (Rev. 20:10). It fits into the context of everything we have mentioned so far about Hell and the end of the world.

Judgment Day will be a day of wrath, not a day of celebration or vindication. It is a day to be feared, especially by those who pay little or no attention to the overall message of the Bible. Remember, "It is a fearful thing to fall into the hands of the living God" (Heb. 10:31).

But very few people worry about this. "Religion is a drag. Priests and ministers are messing up every time you pick up a paper or turn on the TV. If they don't worry about it, then why should I?"

Why…? Because the Bible says you should. But then, the Bible might not be true. But can you afford to take that chance? Do you honestly consider the book nothing more than religious myths and stories that have been collected over the years and put together in book form to give civilization some kind of moral compass?

If you do, then don't worry about any of this stuff. Go off and do your thing. Don't worry about any Day of Judgment.

But consider this: There once lived One who raised the dead and who was raised from the dead himself. (Sounds like someone worth listening to, right?) He said there would be a Day of Judgment and described it this way:

"All the nations will be gathered before Him, and He will separate them one from another, as a shepherd divides his sheep from the goats. And He will set the sheep on His right hand, but the goats on the left. Then the King will say to those on His right hand 'Come, you blessed of My Father, inherit the kingdom prepared for you from the foundation of the world'....Then He will say to those on the left hand 'Depart from me, you cursed, into the everlasting fire prepared for the devil and his angels" (Matt. 25:32-34,41).

You can pooh-pooh that if you want, but the fact that you may be right is a real long shot. You are literally playing with fire in more ways than one.

Try this one on for size. This scene is known as The Great White Throne Judgment. It's for the losers, those who have been found guilty because of their sins, and who now await sentencing.

"And I saw the dead, small and great, standing before God, and books were opened. And another book was opened, which is the Book of Life. And the dead were judged according to their works, by the things that were written in the books.

"The sea gave up the dead who were in it, and Death and Hades delivered up the dead who were in them. And they were judged, each one according to his works.

"And anyone not found written in the Book of Life was cast into the lake of fire" (Rev. 20:12,13,15).

I don't know about you, but that is enough to literally scare the "Hell" out of me. If there are any Books around with lists of good guys, I want to make sure I'm in there. I can't stand the heat in Florida, never mind any lake of fire.

Keep in mind it is Jesus who will do this judging of the wicked (John 5:22). Those who have been saved will not come to this judgment (John 5:24).

Jesus, who healed the lame, who fed the hungry, who gave sight to the blind, this Jesus, whom much of the world has made into this planet's No.1 Good Guy of all time (providing they keep a lid on most of what He said)--it is this Jesus who will cast the majority of mankind into a fiery Hell.

Shouldn't this make us think of Him a bit differently than we have in the past? Shouldn't this give us a better perspective of what this is all about? Shouldn't this tell us that Jesus Christ is not some soft touch whom we need not take too seriously?

It should.

Consider the parable of the wedding feast in Matt. 22:1-14. Jesus starts off by telling us, "The kingdom of heaven is like…" meaning, "This is the way we operate. Everything that follows is the way my Father and I do things." To miss this is to miss the main point of the story.

In this parable it is obvious that the King is God. If the kingdom of heaven is like the following, then the way this king acts is the way God acts. There is no way you can deny this and be honest with the text.

The king throws a big wedding for his son. But those invited decide they don't want to attend. They have better things to do. They even beat up the king's servants and kill them.

What does the king do? He sends out his armies, kills those who were invited but did not come, and burns down their city!

This is one angry king. This is a king you do not cross. Mafia godfathers do not retaliate to this extent. This king demands respect and gets it—or else. (Keep in mind that the kingdom of heaven is like this. Jesus said so.)

The king now invites everyone he can find. He is throwing a party and he wants guests present. Eventually the wedding hall is filled with guests, both good and bad. But one guy shows up without a proper wedding garment. The king doesn't like this and says to him, "How did you get in here without a wedding garment?"

The guy doesn't know what to say. He's speechless.

Now comes the chilling part of the story. The part that is usually ignored because the commentator or preacher is too busy telling us about the actual makeup of the wedding garment, or what is represents, or why you need one, or wedding customs at that time, whatever.... But by concentrating on this they miss the main point of the parable, which is, "The kingdom of heaven is like," meaning, this is the way we operate. The main issue here is not the garment, but rather the king's attitude and point of view.

Jesus is not telling this parable to make a fashion statement about wedding garments. He is telling us this because He wants us to know what we will be facing if we don't do things right, and to plan accordingly so we won't end up like this poor guy who in another minute is going to wish he had never met this king.

If I had been this king I would have been inclined to say to my servants, "Hey, fellas, why don't you take this guy into the back room and get him a proper wedding garment. He might feel somewhat embarrassed in that thing he's wearing." And then I would have said to the man, "Follow them and they'll take care of you. Then go out and join the wedding and have a good time."

I would have been inclined to do something like that. But then, I'm an old softy. I bend with the flow. You can cut a few corners with me.

But you obviously cannot cut any corners with this king. When he invites you to a function you had better come. And when you come you had better be clothed properly. If everything is not done just the way he wants you will be tied up, taken for a ride, and then thrown into outer darkness where there will be weeping and gnashing of teeth. And all because you would not follow simple rules and commands. You insisted upon doing everything your way, and you cared nothing about what the kingdom of heaven was like or what it demanded.

Of course, if you are a believer in Christ, if you have repented of your sins and received Jesus Christ into your heart as Lord and savior, this would not apply to you. You heard the way of salvation proclaimed, acted upon it, and were sealed with the Holy Spirit to await the day of full redemption (Eph. 1:13,14). You know where you stand and where you are going.

You know that the Bible is "...the testimony that God has given us eternal life, and this life is in His son." And that, "He who has the Son has life; he who does not have the Son of God does not have life. These things I have written to you who believe in the name of the Son of God, that you may know that you have eternal life..." (1st John 5:11-13).

The choice is simple and clear. You can play all the games you want with silly theories about reincarnation, evolution, nirvana, atheism, the cessation of life after death, investigating Islam, all religions lead to God, you are loved unconditionally, a God of love would never send anyone to Hell, one church is just as good as another, blah, blah, blah.

You can do that if you like. There is no law that says you can't be a loser too. We have freedom of religion in this country and you can believe whatever you want, and fashion in your mind any God you want.

But, if the Bible is really true as it is written, then none of what we have just listed above can be true. And if that is not true...and the Bible really is true, and you are not tuned into it....

Then believe me—you are in deadly peril and should move fast to correct your situation. There is a verse in James 1:21 that reads, "Therefore lay aside all filthiness and overflow of wickedness, and receive with meekness the implanted word, which is able to save your souls."

Do it, and for the sake of your own soul don't wait a day longer!

That "word" mentioned here is the message of the cross. It is telling you to turn from your sins and turn to Christ. When the truth of Jesus Christ then becomes implanted in your soul you will live. Ignore or reject Him—and you will die the living death of an eternal Hell.

The choice is yours.

A Tragic Tale Of One Man's Indecision

The Man moved slowly across the street, avoiding the slush puddles, and headed for Whacky Jackie's Diner. He did not go right inside, but stopped and looked in through the window. The place was about half filled. He looked at his watch. Twelve-fifty on the nose. He glanced quickly up and down the street, and then went inside.

He sat down in the second booth from the end, beside the window. He knew that his target, Big Frank Gardella, would take the first booth at approximately one o'clock as he did every Friday afternoon. Whacky Jackie, a friend of Big Frank, always made sure that booth was available for him.

The waitress came and said to The Man, "What'll it be?"

The Man scanned the menu. The waitress waited. "Gimme the corned beef on rye," The Man said, "and, uhh…how 'bout a coffee?"

"Okay," the waitress said as she spun away.

The Man again looked at his watch. Twelve fifty-five. It was warm in the diner and The Man debated whether or not he should take off his overcoat. He finally decided against it.

He looked out of the window thinking he might see Big Frank, but instead he saw on the opposite corner a street preacher holding a Bible and speaking in earnest to a small group of people.

The Man shook his head. He had seen people like this all his life. They were as much a part of the city as its wailing sirens, marches for various causes, peace demonstrations, and young black kids with baggy pants and baseball hats on backwards. He hated guys white or black who wore baseball hats backwards, and always had an urge to slap them silly. It was an insult to the game.

The Man focused on the preacher. How could these guys get so excited about something no one could really prove? What motivated them? And what difference did it all make anyway? And who really knew if there was a God? If there was, well…he went to church once or twice a year. He wasn't a real atheist like some guys he knew. And he wasn't as bad as some of them either. He remembered hearing about how the former wrestler Biggie Small had broken an old Korean woman's arm when she wouldn't tell him where her son was hiding out. He wouldn't have done a thing like that. Some guys were worse than animals.

Suddenly the door opened and Big Frank Gardella stepped into the diner. The Man saw this in the large mirror on the back wall. He tensed and automatically felt for the .38 in his shoulder holster. Big Frank turned and walked down to the end booth, passing The Man. He took off his coat and hung it on a peg, then sat down facing The Man.

Big Frank did not know The Man, as The Man had been hired from out of town. But The Man had seen pictures of Big Frank, and had been filled in on his modus operandi. The Man had the advantage.

Then from deep inside it came, like a fist plowing through his innards. The Man grimaced and leaned forward. He was going to reach for his pills, but then decided against it. He had gone over this job a dozen times in his head and thought it best not to change anything.

But this was bad. They had opened him up, taken one look, decided it was hopeless, and had sewn him back up. What had they told him, six months… maybe less? He didn't remember. But he did know the pain was becoming more frequent. Lousy cancer. Why him?

It eased off a bit and The Man began to breathe easier. He then began wondering why he had even taken this job. In six months the big C would have him in his grave. So who needed this?

But then he remembered. The sound of his sister Sheila's voice "...but I don't have the money for David's operation. And those blood-sucking doctors won't do a thing if you don't have medical insurance."

"Look, I'll get the money," he said. "Don't worry."

"You've got enough troubles of your own," she said. "I can't be asking you for money."

"Hey, that kid is important to me too, y'know. I want to see that leg of his straightened out just as much as you do. If he's gonna play Little League next year he's gotta have it done. So don't worry about the bills. I'll take care of them."

With the money from this job, added to some he had saved, he could do it. Fifteen grand to kill Frank Gardella, and who knows, little Davey might someday make the big leagues.

Somebody moved into the booth behind The Man. It was the street preacher, and there was another guy with him. Then the waitress brought the sandwich and coffee he had almost forgotten about. The Man caught himself. He was getting too distracted. Keep your mind on what you're doing, he told himself. This is no time to get careless.

From behind him, "...so I've done some things I shouldn't have done. But I never stole anything big or killed anybody."

"Whatever your sins might be, unless you repent you'll end up in Hell."

"Even though I've led a pretty good life compared to most people?"

"Yes, because a pretty good life doesn't quite make it. The Bible says that all have sinned and fallen short of the glory of God. That includes you. And that's why you need a savior."

The Man grunted to himself. How many times had he heard this stuff? Don't these guys ever quit? Why don't they stick with preaching to old ladies at church socials and leave other people alone? If he wasn't on a job he would have turned around and told the guy to shut up.

The Man looked up and caught Frank Gardella's eyes after Gardella had given his order to the waitress. Gardella looked at him with no expression. The Man turned his head slightly and glanced out of the window. By now Crazy Leo should have the car parked in the alley behind the diner. Two shots, one to the head, one to the heart, and the job would be over. Then he bolts for the rear door and out into the alley and into the car, never again to return to this city. He took a bite of his sandwich and a sip of coffee.

"…always thought Hell was a myth."

"It's no myth. The ungodly will perish in Hell with the Devil and his angels."

"And Jesus died to save me from this?"

"That's right. Salvation is a free gift. It's something God offers you through Christ. You'd be foolish to refuse it."

The Man—surprising himself—suddenly considered this. Would he go to Hell because he killed people…even if some of them were rats and deserved it? He had never seriously thought about this. But maybe the guy behind him didn't know what he was talking about. Most of those guys were fanatics anyway. But then again…

The pain returned. The Man gave a soft groan and shifted his body weight to one side. He glanced up and saw Big Frank Gardella watching him, probably wondering what was going on.

The waitress brought Big Frank's order and he began to eat, still watching The Man.

"…I don't want to die and go to Hell."

"Then repent of your sins and ask the Lord to forgive you and save you. Receive Christ and trust Him as your savior."

The Man clenched his teeth in pain as he listened. If there was a Hell he didn't want to go there either. Maybe he could find another way to get some money to Sheila. He had a couple of things he could sell that he wouldn't be needing anymore, and there were a few guys who owed him some dough. Yeah, there had been enough killing. He could give back the half he had already been paid. They could get someone else.

He was beginning to sweat heavily. The inside of his shirt felt clammy…and the pain was still there.

"The Bible says it is a fearful thing to fall into the hands of the living God…" the preacher was saying. "Whatever a man sows, that he will reap."

"Maybe I have been living pretty much like a fool. Maybe it's time I really got straightened out with God."

Yeah, I don't need this, The Man said to himself. I don't want to die with no more blood on my hands. And what if there really is a Hell? Maybe this preacher guy is right after all. Maybe I should talk to him, find out a little bit more about what he's selling. What have I got to lose? I'm gonna die soon anyway.

The pain began to grow in intensity. The Man knew he would have to take the medicine to get some relief. He looked at Big Frank Gardella. Gardella was eating slowly and watching him. Frank Gardella had been in the mob for over twenty years. He knew his way around, and he knew how to survive.

And he knew trouble when he saw it. There was something in the way The Man was acting that convinced Big Frank that something wasn't right here. He was now on edge.

The Man finalized his decision. He was through with killing. He wasn't going to do it. He would take two of his pills and get out of here. The heck with the preacher guy for now. He was probably crazy like all the rest of them anyway. That stuff could wait. Right now he just wanted to get out of here and get home to his bed. He reached inside his coat pocket…

Big Frank Gardella knew nothing about medicine, or about what the Bible said, or about deep pain in his gut. But he did know that hit men carried their piece in a shoulder holster. When he saw The Man reach inside his coat he knew he would have to move fast.

Frank Gardella leaped to his feet and pulled out a small revolver. He pointed it at The Man.

The Man half rose from his seat. "No, wait…" he said, grabbing for his pills.

Gardella, his eyes filled with sudden fear, pulled the trigger. The lead slug pierced The Man's lungs and sent him sprawling to the floor. People screamed, a few dived under their tables, and someone dropped dishes that crashed to the floor.

Gardella jammed the gun back inside his suit jacket, grabbed for his coat, and ran for the rear door. The street preacher, lifting his head and seeing The Man gasping on the floor, immediately scrambled to his side.

"Hang on," he said to The Man. "An ambulance will be here soon."

From the back alley came the sound of two shots. Everyone inside the diner froze. The Man wondered if Crazy Leo had gotten hit. He made a feeble reach for the preacher's shirt. "I…need…"

"What…what do you need?" the preacher said, bending closer to The Man.

"I…wasn't…going to…." The Man breathed, blood now seeping from the corner of his mouth. "I…"

"Yes, yes…you weren't going to what…?" the preacher asked.

The Man struggled to speak again, but could not. Then the preacher saw tears forming in The Man's eyes. The Man was crying.

And then he died.

-00-